HANCOCK SHAKER VILLAGE / THE CITY OF PEACE

Cover: an 1835 painting of Hancock Shaker Village, acquired for the Village collection from Mrs. M.E. Austin, formerly Sister Olive Hayden of Hancock Shaker Village.

HANCOCK SHAKER VILLAGE / THE CITY OF PEACE

An Effort
To Restore A Vision
1960-1985

By Amy Bess Miller

Library of Congress Number 83-81063
ISBN 0-9613555-0-6

Copyright © 1984 by Hancock Shaker Village,
Hancock, Massachusetts. All rights reserved.

Printed in U.S.A. by the Studley Press,
Dalton, Massachusetts.

To Lawrence Kelton Miller who in 1960 favored the idea of restoring this Shaker Village, turning his interest into serious and sustained coaching and enduring support.

— Hancock, Massachusetts, 1984

Shakers of the Church Family, Hancock, Mass., 1885.

CONTENTS

Acknowledgements / IX

Introduction / 11

Prologue / 15

Restoration / 32

Collections / 98

Trustees, Friends, Council of Friends / 105

Events and Visitations / 110

Major Donors / 133

Publications and Publicity / 139

Professional Personnel and Staff / 145

The Future of the City of Peace / 157

Chronology of Restoration / 162

Appendix (Trustees) / 164

Bibliography / 167

Index / 168

Spirit drawing in the collection, Hancock Shaker Village.

ACKNOWLEDGEMENTS

Several years ago John Calkins of Boston, a trustee of Hancock Shaker Village and chairman of the Long Range Planning Committee, suggested that a history be written to acknowledge the help of others and document the restoration of the Village since it was purchased from the Shakers in 1960.

This has been accomplished, thanks to his interest and the full support and input of all the trustees, the staff and in particular the generous and sympathetic encouragement of Vice President Veola Lederer.

Any omissions are inadvertent, and any errors in the text are mine. In bringing this to press, I was assisted immeasurably by the competent editing and innovative suggestions of Walter Howard and Robert B. Kimball, who was the Village's first volunteer director of public relations.

My thanks go also to the 1982 typing class at St. Joseph's Central High School, in Pittsfield, who typed this manuscript under the direction of Sister Norina Mastro.

A.B.M.

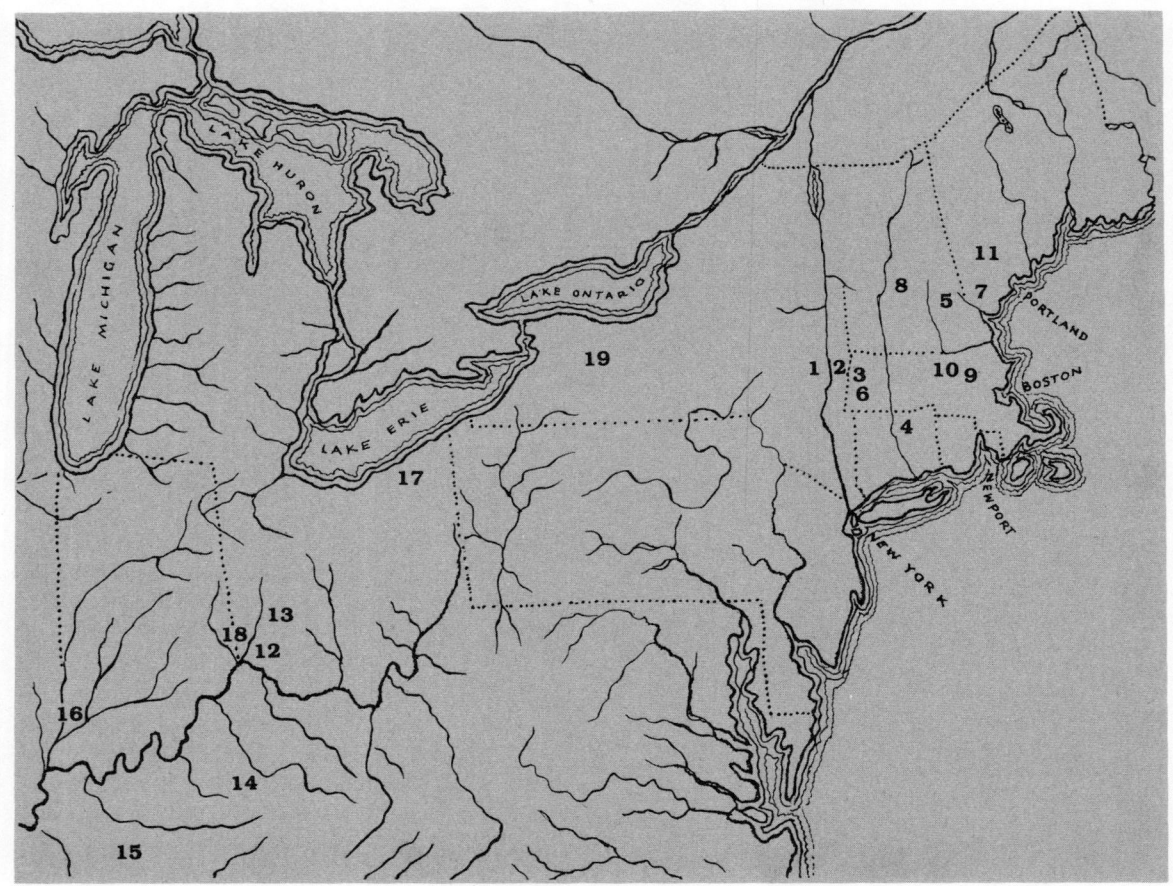

Locations of the Chief Shaker Communities

1. Watervliet, N.Y., 1787-1938
2. Lebanon, N.Y., 1787-1947
3. Hancock, Mass., 1790-1960
4. Enfield, Conn., 1790-1917
5. Canterbury, N.H., 1792-.
6. Tyringham, Mass., 1792-1875
7. Alfred, Me., 1793-1932
8. Enfield, N.H., 1793-1923
9. Harvard, Mass., 1793-1918
10. Shirley, Mass., 1793-1908
11. Gloucester (Sabbathday Lake), Me., 1794-.
12. Union Village, Ohio, 1806-1912
13. Watervliet, Ohio, 1806-1910
14. Pleasant Hill, Ky., 1806-1910
15. South Union, Ky., 1807-1922
16. West Union, Ind., 1810-1827
17. North Union, Ohio, 1822-1889
18. Whitewater, Ohio, 1824-1907
19. Groveland, N.Y., 1826-1895

INTRODUCTION

Ann Lee, the second child in a family of 10 children, was born in Manchester, England, on February 29, 1736. Her father, John Lee, was a blacksmith. Like other children reared in poor families, Ann had no education and was sent to work early — first in a textile mill, then in the hatter's trade, later as a cook in a Manchester hospital.

In 1762, Ann reluctantly acceded to her father's wishes and married one of his apprentices, Abraham Stanley (or Standerin) in the Collegiate Church of Christ near her Manchester home. She bore him four children, all of whom died in infancy or early childhood. This recurrence of tragedy strengthened an already deep conviction that marriage catered to man's carnal nature. In later years, this conviction became the well-known Shaker dogma of celibacy.

Before she married, Ann Lee had become acquainted with a group of dissident Quakers in the nearby village of Bolton. She joined James and Jane Wardley and their small band in the 1750s, soon becoming the acknowledged leader of the group. The Believers, as they called themselves, did not court harassment; neither did they shrink from it. Persecution came early and often, while Ann Lee still lived in Manchester. The constabulary came many times in response to calls from neighbors of the Believers who complained of the noise made by these zealotic people as they sang and danced ecstatically until early morning.

The climax came one Sunday when these "Shaking Quakers," as the public derisively called the United Society of Believers, broke up regular services in Christ Church, Manchester. The vergers called the police, who promptly jailed Ann Lee (she had already barely escaped conviction for heresy, no light charge in those days). While in prison, she had a revelation — belatedly, her neighbors thought — that her destiny and that of her disciples lay in a more tolerant America. Soon after her release, she and eight followers took ship for the promised land, and after a stormy three-month voyage they arrived in New York in August 1744.

Once ashore, the small group of Shakers found lodgings in and around New York City and went to work at their various trades to support themselves. John Hocknell, an emigrant with some money, traveled up the Hudson to Albany, New York, where he rented a tract of land from Stephen van Rensselaer IV, patroon of the manor of Rensselaerwyck. There, the first Shakers in America built a small log cabin as a home for Mother Ann and the Believers, and another cabin to serve as a meeting house.

The mid-1770s were not a propitious time for Englishmen with peculiar ideas to come to a land torn apart by armed revolt against England, the mother country. So it is not surprising that Mother Ann and most of her young followers were again promptly jailed, first in nearby Albany and then in Poughkeepsie. Calmer heads prevailed eventually, and she "and the Elders with her" were allowed to return to their new home at Niskayuna, New York.

In 1781, a "gift" was received by Mother Ann which commanded her to begin missionary labors in lower New England: several towns in Massachusetts, New Lebanon, New York, and some northern Connecticut settlements. Converts came readily. The Great Awakening, as it was known, fueled by the teachings of Jonathan Edwards, George Whitefield and later by the Baptists and Congregationalists (the "New Lights" or Separatists), brought scores of converts to the infant Shaker Church. Indeed, at Canterbury, N.H., most of the Rev. Benjamin Randall's Free Will Baptist congregation left him to join the Believers, to his vast distress.

Mother Ann arrived at Hancock, Massachusetts, in August of 1783, two years after she had first set forth from Niskayuna on her pilgrimage to Hancock and the neighboring towns of Richmond and Pittsfield. The Shaker settlements at

Mount Lebanon, Church Family c. 1890.

Hancock and in neighboring New Lebanon, New York, were established before Mother Ann returned to Niskayuna that fall.

Ann and her brother, Father William, died a year later, in 1784, but the influx of converts to Shakerism continued. Indeed, the often vicious persecution inflicted upon the Shakers only strengthened their faith: "The blood of the martyrs is the seed of the Church." And members of the still-young Shaker communities moved out toward America's frontiers to found new colonies.

By the turn of the century, the lean times were over; prosperous farmers with rich farmland and timberland joined the Believers. A second wave of converts came to the Church in the mid-1840s with the failure of the Millerite expectations that the Last Days had arrived and that Jesus Christ would return in all His glory as He had promised. This coincided with a period of intense spiritualist manifestations and activity among Shakers known as "Mother Ann's Work."

According to Shaker dogma, Jesus and Mother Ann were both wholly human, but both ordained of the Christ Spirit (the Holy Ghost) for the redemption of mankind. Mother Ann was thought to be Christ (*not* Jesus, be it noted) reincarnated for the particular redemption of female humanity which had fallen from grace because of the concupiscent Eve. As the saviors were dual, so was the Godhead — Almighty God and Holy Mother Wisdom. This duality of deity was and still is part of Shaker, Mormon and particularly Christian Science theology.

As a result of these two waves of conversion, 12 communities of Shakers were established in the Northeast: two in Maine, two in New Hampshire, four in Massachusetts, one in Connecticut and three in New York. In addition, spurred on by the great Kentucky revival movement of the early 19th century, two communities were established there and four in Ohio, with one short-lived settlement in Indiana — the West as the Shakers and other Americans then knew it.

At its peak around 1849, the order was estimated to have between six and ten thousand members — men, women, and children. There were many children, both offspring of convert parents and adopted orphans. For these youngsters, schools were established with brethren and sisters as instructors. The boys went to school in winter, when there was less farm work, and the girls in early summer.

A decline in members of the Shaker Order which began in the mid-19th century was disastrously accelerated during the Civil War. To modern Americans, exposed usually for the first time to the doctrine of celibacy, lack of propagation is the obvious explanation for this decline. Celibacy was not popular among lay Protestants; unlike the Catholic orders, which could recruit members from a large Catholic laity, the Shakers had to contend with a Protestant population basically antipathetic to their principles.

More important, the lure of the materialistic world with its glitter, its paid wages and its set hours of labor, presented a major obstacle to recruitment. The overwhelming reason for the decline of the Society was industrialization. Further, of all the children whom the Shakers reared, fewer than 10 per cent continued on in life as Shakers.

It is true that the Shakers operated many highly profitable industries, but first and always they were farmers. Shaker industry was only a by-product of their basic agricultural communalism. As such, these industries could not compete successfully with worldly businesses whose sole purpose was to manufacture specialized products. The last of the Shaker industries were the famous chair-manufacturing operations and the production of pharmaceuticals, which ended around 1935.

Yet another reason for the Shaker decline is an indirect by-product of the Industrial Revolution. As sounder banks and stronger industrial systems came into existence, they occupied more and more of men's attention and interest, to the detriment of religious preoccupations. Fewer adults were converted to the Shaker way of life to replace those Believers who died. Then, too, state and municipal authorities took over the care of orphan children, thereby diminishing the opportunity for Shakers to influence and to recruit young people to their way of life. It was a losing battle, no matter how hard the brethren struggled to reverse the trend.

The last quarter of the 19th and the first of the 20th centuries witnessed the demise of community after community. First to go was Tyringham, Massachusetts, in 1875, followed by North Union, Ohio (1889), Groveland, New York (1895), Watervliet, Ohio (1910), Whitewater, Ohio, (1907), Shirley, Massachusetts, (1908), Pleasant Hill, Kentucky, (1910), Union Village, Ohio, (1912), Enfield, Connecticut (1917), Enfield, New Hampshire (1923), Harvard, Massachusetts (1918), South Union, Kentucky (1922), Alfred, Maine (1932), Watervliet, New York (1938), Mount Lebanon, New York (1947), and Hancock, Massachusetts (1960). Two communities still exist: Canterbury, New Hampshire, with three sisters (including two Ministry Eldresses), and Sabbathday Lake, Maine, with five sisters.

Of the defunct villages, several have been taken over by religious orders or are used as hospitals. One is partly owned by a private school and three — Pleasant Hill, South Union, Kentucky and Hancock, Massachusetts — are museum restorations. The rest are in private hands.

What is the future of the United Society of Believers? In 1957, by action of the Ministry, the rolls were closed and further recruitment ceased. Both Canterbury and Sabbathday Lake have created nonprofit corporations to which their properties have been deeded, with the provision that the remaining Sisters have the right of domicile so long as they wish it. Here, and at the restorations in Pleasant Hill, South Union and Hancock, the preservation of the buildings and artifacts is assured, and the Shaker way of life will be presented to future generations — lasting tributes to the oldest and longest-lived of all the many communal experiments in this country.

The Shaker ideals of simplicity, honesty, hard work, abandonment of war, belief in a directing deity and love of neighbor will endure and inspire men and women of future generations, though the Believers themselves will not then be with us. Shakerism and its message will therefore never die.

Robert F. W. Meader

Shaker girls doing calisthenics.

PROLOGUE

The following pages will explain, I hope, how my consuming interest in the Shakers, particularly the Hancock community, developed. It was largely by happenstance. In fact, as I shall tell, contact with the New Hampshire Shakers started in childhood. Later as a schoolgirl, I was visually conscious of their culture in another New England setting. As a bride, I first met and conversed with nearby Shaker sisters in Western Massachusetts in still another community, even as the order was in irreversible decline. Accidental exposure meanwhile to Shaker scholarship deepened the interest. The calendar then took over. So 38 years after my first exposure, I became part of a corporate entity formed to preserve at least the physical, if not the spiritual, assets of this ever-fascinating society.

First, however, let me set the stage visually.

When land in the Berkshires of Western Massachusetts was largely devoted to farming, roughly 3,000 acres on both sides of the Boston-Albany post road, now U.S. Route 20, was Shaker land. Once the traveler was five miles west of Pittsfield's Town Hall, he could sense the land had a different look. This difference was in the well-fenced meadows, the large stands of pine on the upland slopes, the tidy sugarbush and the neat 10-acre fields interrupted by hillocks and bounded by gentle ridges.

Continuing westward over the Taconic Range of mountains into New York State once again the traveler had a feeling of being in another country. For this also was Shaker land — 6,000 acres of it at one time belonging to another Shaker community whose holdings were contiguous to the Massachusetts settlement.

As a teen-ager in the late '20s at a Pittsfield boarding school going by bus occasionally to Albany for some cultural function, I can remember the driver's slowing down as we approached the Hancock Shakers and pointing out the buildings that he knew about firsthand. His father had worked for the Shakers as a carpenter, and from him he had come to appreciate their fine workmanship. He was proud of the Round Stone Barn, always referred to by the Shakers as the "circular barn."

As our bus churned over Lebanon Mountain into New York state and adjusted to curves on the downgrade, our driver would slow down once we were on the plain and have us look back at the Mount Lebanon Shaker barn high on the hillside. It was indeed a formidable sight, even viewed at a distance across the valley. This magnificent stone five-story dairy barn was, our driver told us, the largest for miles around. To make it even more interesting to us who knew so little about cows, he said that each stall had the cow's name above it. Then he would recite the names — Rose, Ruby, Daisy, Pearl, Jennie, Nellie, Ruth, Becky, Bessie, Baby and so on. There were more than 50 of them.

Homeward bound, coming eastward after a concert, a play, a lecture or whatever occasioned our outing, whether the evening was moonlit or not, that big pale stone barn and the smaller light-grey circular stone barn at Hancock shone forth as an unforgettable presence.

A friend, now a trustee, who made a round trip to Camp Drum, New York, for National Guard duty each summer, said he was invariably awed as he approached the Shaker Village at Hancock, especially if it were growing dark and the buildings were lighted, faintly he thought, as if by candles or kerosene lamps. Day or night, there was an air of serenity, order, simplicity, but still projecting was the restless thrust of earth's fertility.

The same atmosphere prevails at three other Shaker Villages now open to the public. Pleasant Hill, Kentucky, which I have visited over the years, is quite different physiographically. Here there is a feeling of more open country with finely constructed "stone fences," or zigzagging split-rail fences enclosing spacious bluegrass meadows. But the same sense of order prevails.

At Sabbathday Lake, Maine, one comes upon the Shaker Village strung along a straight stretch of road with its trim buildings of clapboard and the white Meeting House, set in a luxuriant apple orchard across the road from a spacious herb garden.

A similar sense prevails at Canterbury, New Hampshire, but the traveler does not come upon it suddenly. He first sees the village at the top of a hill, from a distance of perhaps a mile. There is a certain freshness about the land; the ground looks richer, the grass greener, and the buildings are neatly spaced with their dooryards framed by large maples and apple trees. As of this writing, I have visited 16 of the 19 other Shaker sites, two of which were short-lived communes.

Once when I motored with Julia Neal, a Shaker scholar, in Kentucky to see for the first time the Shaker Village at South Union, I asked how far away we were and she told me I would know the minute we came to "Shakerland." And indeed when we came to neat, straight fences, although then unpainted, bordering fields mowed exactly to the tree lines, where the farm roads, although out of regular use, were still straight and unrutted — and certainly when the great center Dwelling House, then uninhabited and in need of repair, came upon the horizon — I knew we were in "Shakerland."

At Hancock the six "families" numbering 217 souls in 1846 had diminished in the 1930s to one, the Church Family. Hired men helped the few surviving brothers with their chores. The fields and some of the barns had been rented to neighboring farmers. Visibly, the property was running down, showing signs of declining order, but still the sense of past fructification remained.

Shortly after I returned to Pittsfield in 1933 as a bride, my father-in-law drove me over Lebanon Mountain, known as Holy Mount to the Shakers, to call on his friends, Eldress Emma Neale and her blood sister, Sister Sadie Neale, the garden deaconess, and also a trustee. Another Shaker friend of his at Mount Lebanon was Eldress Sarah Collins, the community's sole surviving chairmaker. My father-in-law had known them for years and had often edited their letters to *The Berkshire Eagle*, the local newspaper of which he was editor and publisher. They liked to make known their views on political issues although they did not vote. This rule was broken once, however, when they registered to vote for congressional candidates favoring the Volstead Act, which was the federal law enforcing the 18th (Prohibition) Amendment.

One lovely spring day in April on such a trip we left the Pittsfield-Albany highway (U.S. Route 20) and slowly approached the center of the Mount Lebanon Shaker Village under a bower of elms and maples, pale green and pink in bud. Ahead of us in the middle of the dirt road sat a man on a chair with a gun across his knees. Mr. Miller did not slow down and continued to describe the land and buildings to left and right. Finally I said, "Oh, do stop; that man isn't going to get out of your way." "He will," was the reply and, of course, he did.

When we talked with Eldress Emma later, Mr. Miller asked who her "guardian" was and inquired if he was always there in the middle of the road. The gentle old lady said softly, "Yea, he protects us." Later we learned that at night he let his friends into the Village and they helped themselves to any and all salable material not locked up.

The first time I went to call on the Hancock Shakers with Mr. Miller we inspected Brother Ricardo Belden's new car, either a Reo or a Buick; I am not sure which. The car was always referred to as "his" car, as he was its only driver.

The Shakers, when needing a new car, had several Pittsfield dealers bring samples to the Village. They had to be dark in color and comfortable for three sisters in the back seat. Curtains of a neutral shade were specified to pull down "against the sun." Tools were taken for granted, but two spare tires and a trunk were required. Brother Ricardo would have a trial spin alone with the salesman and then as his choice narrowed, another ride was arranged with three sisters in the back and Sister Frances Hall in the front with him.

Later, the favored agent would be asked to name his best price in a trade. No Shaker car was driven more than three years, we were told, and its condition was always excellent. A brick garage had been erected near the Trustees' House. It was built with the future and larger membership of the Society in mind, as indicated

A Shaker car. Brother Ricardo Belden is behind the wheel.

Brother Ricardo Belden

Eldress Fanny Estabrook

by the four bays in the little building. One of its practical features was the wrap-around system of steam pipes installed to keep the car engines from freezing in the severe Berkshire winters.

In the opinion of the ever-progressive Shakers, the automobile was one of the great steps forward in modern technology. The first car purchased by the Hancock Church Family was a Cadillac, although they also owned at one time or another a Reo, a Franklin, a Dodge and a Buick. A 1919 newspaper account of a Shaker funeral had noted, "Among the finest cars seen at the Shaker funeral were those owned by the Shakers themselves. All the communities have them now. They go on the theory that the best is invariably the cheapest in the long run."

The Shakers were generous contributors to the Pittsfield Community Fund, as it was known in those days. In the fall of 1936 as a young wife, I was asked to take their subscription card and call on Eldress Fanny Estabrook and Sister Frances Hall at the Trustees' House. I made the appointment and felt well armed with information. However, I wasn't quite prepared for the extensive cross-examination by the two sisters reinforced by Sister Mary Dahm.

We sat in the front parlor under a hanging lamp where 24 years later we would sit again for a different purpose. The questions were gentle, but pertinent. I was told that usually a man came with their card in the evening. I replied that I had a six-month-old baby and had to call while she napped. They were interested in the baby's name and in the fact that our Shaker friends at Canterbury, New Hampshire, which I had first visited as a child growing up in Worcester, Massachusetts, in the 1920s with my mother and aunt, had sent her a fine red cloak which she would eventually grow into. They asked me to bring my new daughter to call on them sometime. Then Sister Frances left the room to bring us some cider and cookies. When she returned she also had a check for the Fund and it represented an increase of twice the amount I had suggested.

Although by this time I had visited the Shakers at Hancock and Mount Lebanon as well as the family at Canterbury many times, it was not until I got to know Dr. and Mrs. Edward Deming Andrews of Pittsfield, noted scholars of Shakerism, that I started buying furniture at Hancock and Lebanon and exploring their barns and dwellings.

My husband and I were building in Pittsfield a house to accommodate a growing family, and we wanted Shaker furniture to be part of it. Its simple lines, its durable construction, its pleasant finish suited our needs and tastes.

With the two Andrewses I made many visits, sometimes to Hancock, but mostly to the Mount Lebanon community. It was a rewarding period, for I got to know the remaining Shaker sisters and to learn their personal histories. Both Dr. and Mrs. Andrews had discerning taste and stimulated my imagination as to the usefulness of the furniture. I was more than just ordinarily enthusiastic; I was totally absorbed, and spent the years from 1937 to 1959 in pursuit of Shaker history and artifacts.

The war years intervened and there were many months when it was impossible to travel to Hancock or over the Taconic Range to Mount Lebanon. Many changes took place, all of them sad. Several buildings at Hancock were removed or dismantled by the Shakers to lighten their tax load, since they sought no exemption or abatement because of their religious status. Their religion was, they said, their way of life and so they paid the going rate on almost 2,000 acres of land and more than 20 buildings.

Of the important buildings razed, the saddest disappearance was that of their Meeting House, which came down in 1938. Each year there were more sheds and outbuildings missing. Sister Mary Frances Hall, the last trustee at Hancock, generally called "Miss" Hall by non-Shakers, but always referred to by the Shakers as Sister Frances, died on March 10, 1957, aged 81. The next year the Sisters' Shop west of the Brick Dwelling, where we had bought candy and fancy goods, was taken down. The following year, on December 2, Brother Ricardo Belden died, 20 days short of his 90th birthday, leaving an ailing eldress and two sisters as the sole remaining Shakers in the community.

Brother Ricardo, the last male Shaker at the Hancock settlement, was memorable for several reasons. There was something of a mystery about him. It was believed by some that he was in reality Charlie Ross — who, as a two-year-old boy of a wealthy family — had mysteriously disappeared in Eastern Massachusetts and had somehow been delivered to the Shakers, who brought him up. This story was denied by the Shakers, as Ricardo and his blood sister, Elizabeth, had come to the Shakers through proper channels, each living in the Community until their deaths as venerable Believers.

Brother Ricardo lived in the Brethren's Shop on the second floor and had his workshop on the first floor, where he repaired clocks and sewing machines. Stuart C. Henry, director emeritus of the Berkshire Museum, and Robert G. Newman, librarian emeritus of the Berkshire Athenaeum, both recall his coming to the museum and the library, respectively, to repair their clocks, always successfully.

With the passing of Brother Ricardo, Hancock's last male Shaker, it is interesting to point out that 100 years before, the Church Family at Hancock, as with most Shaker families, was composed of 100 members with an almost equal division of Shaker brothers and sisters. This harmonious balance was also evident in the housekeeping. A visitor to Hancock during that period had written:

> Everything is in such perfect order and kept so delicately clean and neat that an air of refinement, not to say luxury, seems to pervade...

Contrarily, Nathaniel Hawthorne found this "perfect order" painful. He wrote after his visit to Hancock in 1851:

> Everything so neat that it was a pain and constraint to look at it; especially as it did not imply any real delicacy or moral purity in the occupants of the house.

This "air of refinement" was still evident within the Hancock Trustees' House 100 years later, even though the calendar inexorably pointed to the end of the order. I vividly remember the uncharacteristic wallpaper with saucy life-size red cardinals perched in white dogwood trees on the walls of the office. It covered the traditional white plaster walls of an earlier "classic" period. Nevertheless, there was unmistakable Shaker order present.

In the Village itself, however, the buildings in the period after World War II had grown shabby and forlorn. The fields were sadly neglected. Missing was the slow movement of cows in the rich meadows. Where corn had grown tall, goldenrod now replaced it, hiding rusty barbed-wire fencing. The Shakers were strong and careful administrators dedicated to an orderliness which was not carried out with equal care by superintendents or, in some cases, by nearby farmers who rented their acres.

After the death of Sister Frances Hall, a woman of good business sense who had served as a Hancock Shaker trustee, the problem of management of the Hancock property increased in gravity. As the movement declined in other locations, non-Shaker caretakers or superintendents were hired to live on the premises and carry on the business transactions of renting the fields and barns and selling off for removal the dwellings or small structures no longer in use.

This happened at Hancock. But in the late '50s, it became increasingly difficult to find a resident manager satisfactory to the Central Ministry at Canterbury. The death of Sister Frances Hall was doubtless the last straw which led to the dissolution of the community at Hancock and the decision to sell the property.

There was an earlier indication as to which way the wind was blowing. In January 1959, the Shakers had transferred 550 acres of woodland in the northeast corner of the property, north of Route 20, to the Commonwealth of Massachusetts to add to the acreage of the adjoining Pittsfield State Forest. Deeded over at a modest figure, it became Massachusetts' first memorial to the Believers when the state in return agreed to assume the maintenance of the Shaker cemetery. Eldress Emma B. King, head of the Central Ministry at Canterbury, stated: "The transfer of this land is another step in disposing of outlying lands connected with the Hancock Shaker colony."

In spite of this land sale and other signs and rumors (a "For Sale" sign had appeared on a plot of land at the south end of the Village) that something was in the wind at Hancock, the decision to liquidate the community came abruptly. Attorney Frederick M. Myers in the autumn of 1959, telephoned me that the whole property was being put on the market at once.

The asking price was $200,000, with the sum of $20,000 required for an option.

Some months before the inevitable decision, it became apparent that Hancock's days were numbered. A group calling itself the Hancock Shaker Village Steering Committee had been discussing what might be done in such an eventuality. Those who had been asked to form a committee were: Mr. and Mrs. David V. Andrews, Dr. and Mrs. Edward D. Andrews, Dorothy Miller Cahill, Mrs. Davis T. Dunbar, Mrs. John A. Gilchrist, Professor Henry Russell Hitchcock, Jean Lipman, Mr. and Mrs. Carl P. Rollins, Mr. and Mrs. Milton C. Rose, Frank O. Spinney, and Mrs. and Mrs. Carl A. Weyerhaeuser.

Before the next committee meeting, Amy Bess, Lawrence and Donald Miller called on John S. Williams of Old Chatham, New York, to discuss the situation. John, a "gentleman" dairy farmer, had been an avid and discriminating collector of Shaker material; he had written about the Shakers and had the confidence of the eldresses. He had founded the Shaker Museum in Old Chatham in 1950 and used his spacious barns to exhibit his wide range of Shakerana.

The Millers wanted to be sure that Williams was advised of the imminent sale of the Hancock Community and given the opportunity to refuse the purchase. He stated unequivocally that he wanted his collection to stay where it was, across the road from his residence, and was not interested in any other proposal.

A meeting was called for November 1, 1959, to discuss ways and the means of acquiring and developing the Village. Attending were seven members of the Steering Committee. In a way it was history repeating itself, for it was not the first time a group had pondered forming a society to preserve the physical assets of Shakerism in Berkshire County. This time, though, there was a feeling of great hope.

Twenty-seven years before, in October of 1932, Dr. and Mrs. Andrews had exhibited their Shaker furniture and artifacts at the Berkshire Museum, where the display was well received. Eldress Sarah Collins of Mount Lebanon and Sisters Elizabeth Belden and Alice Smith of Hancock were among the guests. They were quoted in the local newspaper as sympathizing with the desires of Dr. and Mrs. Andrews and the Berkshire Museum to awaken the public to the importance of Shakerism in the cultural, sociological and religious history of this country.

The opening night of the exhibition, John Barker, a trustee of the Berkshire Museum, had introduced the Andrewses and Laura M. Bragg, the Museum's director. He announced that there was a plan afoot for a public meeting to discuss the founding of a society for the preservation of Shaker culture. One of the objectives would be to establish in a central area in an appropriate environment a facility for the safekeeping and display of furniture, artifacts and other Shaker material which the Andrewses had been collecting since the late 1920s. The society would be national in scope.

Dr. and Mrs. Andrews had felt certain there was a growing fascination with Shaker history — evident after exhibitions of their collections outside the Berkshire area, one at the Whitney Museum of American Art, then on West Eighth Street in New York, in 1934, and a second in 1938, at the Worcester (Massachusetts) Art Museum. However, for various reasons nothing further was done to formally consolidate the interest.

Twenty years later the Andrewses had reason to be more optimistic. In 1956 Yale University accepted the entire Andrews collection. Dr. Andrews, a graduate of Amherst College, had received a Ph.D. from Yale in 1939 for his dissertation on the history of Vermont education. He had also been temporary curator of history at the New York State Museum at Albany. In 1937 he had been awarded a Guggenheim fellowship for research in the arts and history of the Shakers. In March of 1937, "Shaker Furniture: The Craftsmanship of an American Communal Sect," by Edward D. and Faith Andrews had been published with the assistance of a grant from the American Council of Learned Societies. It was issued by the Yale University Press and Carl Purington Rollins, Printer to the University, and was enthusiastically received. It was the first major book on the Shakers, their cultural background, their furniture, crafts, houses and shops, illustrated with photographs by William F. Winters.

Dr. Andrews's friends were happy that at last a permanent place had been found at Yale not only for the collection, but also that an academic forum on Shakerism for Dr. Andrews would be established. Yale announced that Dr. and Mrs. Andrews would catalog and document their collection, which would gradually be transferred from their Richmond, Massachusetts, residence, the Berkshire Museum, their New York City apartment and the New York State History Association's Fenimore House in Cooperstown, New York.

Their first exhibition was to be held during the 1957-58 academic year. Dr. Andrews, writing with Mrs. Andrews of his experience as a donor in *Fruits of the Shaker Tree of Life*, described his hopes for the affiliation with Yale and his pleasure in having their work so honored. But at the end of the first year he wrote: "There came a series of events which drastically altered the whole situation ..." As a result the gift was withdrawn.

And so the meeting of the Hancock Shaker Village Steering Committee on November 1, 1959, was crucial and had a double purpose. We wanted Dr. and Mrs. Andrews to find at long last a permanent place for their collections, and we wanted to save and preserve the Village. We were guided by two experienced people — Mrs. Gilchrist, an architectural historian, and Dorothy Miller, curator of collections at the Museum of Modern Art in Manhattan, also a collector of Shaker furniture.

They proposed accomplishing the most difficult task at once: to prepare a statement of purpose. Mrs. Gilchrist thought the restoration of the Village should be conceived as an "outdoor museum" similar to certain folk museums in Europe. She posed the question of ownership: Should the property be held privately until an institution, national or state, or a foundation, could assume control?

Dr. Andrews read a letter from Frank O. Spinney, then director of Old Sturbridge Village and later a trustee of Hancock Shaker Village. Mr. Spinney wrote that he was predisposed toward the educational, nonprofit, trustee-owned type of operation in effect at Old Sturbridge. It was agreed that it would be best to set up this type of operation — an educational institution which would be tax-exempt and which would seek public and foundation support. It was further suggested that Attorney Myers be told that we were seeking tax-exemption and were forming a board of trustees of which the Steering Committee was the nucleus.

Lawrence K. Miller was instructed to tell Mr. Myers that a group of which he was a member was seriously interested in the property and to ask for first refusal. It was decided to invite the following people in addition to the initial group to the next meeting: Loring Conant, director of Trustees of Public Reservations (since renamed the Trustees of Reservations); S. Lane Faison, director of the Williams College Art Museum; Philip Guyol, director of the New Hampshire Historical Society; Richard H. Howland, president of the National Trust for Historic Preservation; Mr. and Mrs. Milton C. Rose and Frank O. Spinney.

Soon after the November meeting our group was informed by the Shaker Ministry that interviews with several organizations and individuals interested in the property would be held at the Trustees' Office at Hancock and we learned from Mr. Myers that our interview would take place January 15, 1960. When a bona fide offer was made, we were told it must include a statement concerning its proposed use.

In the interim, we were sent a description of the property by Richard A. Morse, Esq., a lawyer whose Manchester, New Hampshire firm of Sheehan, Phinney, Bass, Green & Bergevin, represented the Shaker Ministry.

DESCRIPTION

The property consisted of 974 acres — 732 acres north of Route 20 and 242 acres south of the highway. The great bulk of the land was in Hancock, plus 190 acres in Pittsfield. More than half the acreage was wooded. Something over 200 acres were pastureland, and nearly 100 acres were tillage. The property contained a small pond on the ridge north of Route 20 for water supply. There were 11 principal buildings and 10 less-important buildings, covering 10 acres.

With the description came four restrictions and a reverter clause:

1. A restriction against any use in connection with parimutuel gambling or a racetrack.

John Ott, director of Hancock Shaker Village until 1983, at rear. Front, from left, Eldress Bertha Lindsay, Sister Miriam Wall, Eldress Gertrude M. Soule.

2. A restriction against any use as a penal or correctional institution.
3. A restriction against the sale of alcoholic beverages on the premises.
4. There will also be reserved from the premises a small Shaker cemetery and a right-of-way to the same.

The reverter clause stipulated that the property should be used for nonprofit, educational, literary or charitable purposes only, and that in the event the property, or any portion thereof, were used for other purposes the title should revert to the Shaker Ministry. The asking price was $200,000.

Our interview was held in the Trustees' Office in the front parlor. Eldress Emma B. King of Canterbury and Eldress Gertrude M. Soule, then of Sabbathday Lake, Maine, and Sister Ida Crook from Canterbury represented the Central Ministry. John J. Sheehan and Richard A. Morse of Manchester, New Hampshire, Walter Foss of Portland, Maine, and Frederick M. Myers of Pittsfield were their legal representatives. Mr. and Mrs. Lawrence K. Miller with their lawyer, Charles R. Crimmin, represented the would-be buyers. We read our proposal, which was:

> As the first step in a unique program of conserving the artifacts and values of an unusually significant way of life and work we want to acquire the buildings and land and save for the future the Shaker settlement in the conviction that the projected educational activities envisioned (by our group) should be carried on in a setting which bears the aspect and breathes the spirit of the original culture. The property will be restored to give the Village its traditionally neat and orderly appearance. The purity and quiet dignity of Shaker architecture represented at Hancock by the Brick Dwelling, the Round Stone Barn, the Trustees' Office, the Brethren's and Sisters' Shops and other structures, are among the community's greatest assets. After restoration these buildings will house, in increasing degrees, the furnishings of a typical Shaker "family," an unexcelled library documenting this and other communitarian experiments; the tools of Shaker industry, with the products of such tools; and material illustrative of the agricultural economy of the order. (Much of the above will be drawn from the well-known Andrews collection, with careful selections from other private collections.) Certain industries, such as weaving and craftsmanship in wood, will be revived in the shops, and among the outdoor enterprise, an herb garden patterned after the famous "physics" gardens of the society. The office and store will function again for the reception of visitors and as an outlet for whatever products are manufactured. Another Shaker custom will be revived by serving to visitors on weekends a bounteous "family dinner."
>
> The plan is to make the Community, in its physical appearance and historic functioning, a *living* organization. The property is located in a beautiful countryside where visitors will be inspired by the creation of a simple, communal way of life which has always attracted visitors from far and wide.

Several meetings were held with the Shakers to work out details and finally our group offered $125,000 for the property. This price was arrived at after consultation with Laurence R. Connor, president of the Agricultural National Bank, as it was known then, of Pittsfield. Mr. Connor had advised us as each step was taken and he agreed to have the Agricultural Bank loan $125,000 at 4 per cent for the purchase, after we became incorporated and had filed for tax-exempt status.

Mr. Connor became treasurer of the corporation and served for 10 years until his death on November 3, 1970. He felt such a restoration would add greatly to Berkshire cultural life and would in time attract many visitors to the area. His feeling was that such an investment, compared to a new business locating in the region, would not be a burden to the tax base. There would be no demands on the school system. Public-works requirements such as water and sewer would be minimal as would the need for police and fire protection.

Other parties were interested in purchasing the property. At least two of them were willing to meet the asking price of $200,000. Some bidders were easily turned away by the Shakers' antipathy toward racing and the sale of liquor, and the most aggressive of these were connected with the racetrack contiguous to the Village property on the southwest. Later Mr. Morse told us he thought the track representative would probably not go above $150,000.

The Shakers' concern that their property might be used for the extension of parimutuel gambling was a real one. In 1954 the Berkshire County Fair had been set up on a 48-acre plot abutting the Village on the southwest. The acreage was once Shaker land. Actually it was a revival of the Hancock Fair held over the mountain in Hancock Valley by the center of the town. It had succumbed in the '20s. New England agricultural fairs to succeed nowadays, unless they are small operations, must depend on parimutuel betting on horse racing. This had been the experience of the Barrington Fair in the southern part of the county.

Massachusetts law is not too precise on what constitutes an agricultural fair. In addition, by state regulation the division of profits from parimutuel betting at fairs is more favorable to fair promoters than to those who operate commercial tracks. The promoters behind the Berkshire County Fair were given permission to hold seven days of racing in 1954 by the State Racing Commission. This modest racing operation under the aegis of a "paper fair" continued for 26 years with presumably modest profits. Spectators at Hancock in its early days were seated in bleachers along the home stretch of a half-mile track.

In the late 1950s, however, the Shakers felt a more serious threat was posed to their adjoining property. A commercial horse racing operation was proposed for the Berkshire County Fair site when the property was not being used for fair racing. Capital from outside the state was involved and a corporation was formed to operate Berkshire Downs in Hancock. There was vigorous local opposition in hearings before the state Racing Commission on the issuance of racing dates by those who felt commercial racing was out of character with the other recreational and cultural offerings of the Berkshires.

The Racing Commission in 1960, however, awarded the operators of Berkshire Downs 24 days of racing. Carpenters were soon at work erecting a grandstand seating 3,400. Commercial racing nonetheless did not prosper at Berkshire Downs and the last commercial meet was held in 1969. The Berkshire County Fair continued to use the Hancock site for fair racing until 1977, when its promoters transferred their operation to the track in Great Barrington. Meanwhile the Hancock site, now owned by the Rooney sporting interests of Pittsburgh, Pennsylvania, which operate a dog track in Pownal, Vermont, lies vacant, dilapidated and weed-strewn in contrast to the orderly restoration in the adjoining acreage to the northeast.

Our meetings with the Shaker Ministry during the spring and summer of 1960 during negotiations were always pleasant and interesting. As one of our founding trustees, Robert G. Newman, said recently "... looking back over the years it has always been gratifying that from the very beginning the Shakers were with us and wanted us to succeed."

On the afternoon of June 28, 1960, our group made its final presentation and indicated a willingness to accept the three restrictions and the reverter clause, and at its meeting the next day, June 29, 1960, the Ministry took the following step:

> Voted: that the property be sold to the Miller group (for $125,000), in accordance with the terms and agreements reached with that group at yesterday's meeting, and that the attorneys for the Shakers be authorized to work out the detail of the purchase and sale contract to be signed at the next meeting of the Ministry.

At that same meeting on June 29, the Ministry voted to discontinue the Pittsfield-Hancock family as an organized Shaker society and transfer to the Shaker Central Trust Fund in Manchester, New Hampshire, any of its remaining assets after the sale of land and buildings to the Miller group. While never authenticated by the Shakers themselves, it was the consensus of the Pittsfield financial community that several million dollars in cash and securities had been transferred out of Pittsfield to New Hampshire. Thus, the lovely Village founded in 1790 was destined to become a museum, the property of a nonprofit educational corporation.

Perhaps "museum" is not the proper word, for what the founders envisioned was not a collection of isolated objects but rather a complete and entire representation of Shaker life in an authentic setting. It would be an original and almost totally integrated community, authentic in every respect and preserved substantially as it was in its finest hour.

The venture had the approval of the Shakers themselves as Eldress Emma B. King, head of the Society at Canterbury, New Hampshire, stated:

> The Shakers must now dispose of their village properties in Pittsfield and Hancock since only three members of the local society remain, and it is no longer possible to maintain the Shaker buildings in the fine condition which has been a Shaker tradition.
>
> In disposing of the properties of discontinued Shaker societies, the Parent Ministry has always been especially anxious that these lands and buildings be devoted to some use which is charitable or educational and of benefit to the community. While there is naturally a feeling of regret at closing up a Shaker home of over a century and a half, our regret is tempered by the knowledge that our physical properties will serve some purpose of benefit to mankind after we have left them.
>
> It is therefore a satisfaction and a joy to us that the group which will now assume these properties at Hancock will use them for the preservation of the Shaker traditions and the education of others in the Shaker crafts and industries.
>
> The three remaining members, all of whom are of advancing years, will remain in the Pittsfield area, but will be in communication with the remaining Shaker societies in Maine and New Hampshire and will be cared for under the supervision of the Shaker Parent Ministry.

Steps were taken at once to form a corporation and draw up bylaws. These were prepared by Attorney Charles R. Crimmin of Pittsfield, who became a founding member of the Board of Trustees. They were such useful instruments that in more than 20 years the bylaws have never been amended.

At the incorporators' meeting on August 15, 1960, were: Bernard R. Carman, Charles R. Crimmin, Stuart C. Henry, Patricia A. Lynch (now Mrs. Frank M. Faucett), Paul J. Major, Amy Bess Williams Miller, Lawrence K. Miller, Margo Miller and Robert G. Newman. The corporation was chartered by the Commonwealth of Massachusetts on August 19, 1960.

One of our most generous and enthusiastic friends and advisers in the days following the takeover was C. Lambert Heyniger, headmaster of the Darrow School at the Mount Lebanon Shaker Village. "Lam," as he was affectionately known, had supervised the remodeling of 16 Shaker buildings adapted for boarding-school use during the 22 years he was headmaster. No one knew better than he what lay ahead of us, and yet not once did he sound a discouraging note. It was a sad day for us when he died at his home October 29, 1960, after a long siege of cancer.

A letter shortly before his death designated certain Shaker artifacts he wanted to come to Hancock from the holdings at Mount Lebanon. Many pieces of furniture owned by the school were eventually put up at auction, but Mr. Heyniger's trustees honored a letter from him to our trustees, and several very special and unique articles were given to the Village.

Outstanding among these were two roadside crosses, erected in 1842 outside the Meeting House at New Lebanon, as it was called until 1861, when the name was changed to Mount Lebanon. These crosses warned that the Sabbath services would be closed to the public. Before that, for several years, the meetings had admitted the public. The Ministry reopened the meetings in 1845. The crosses are exhibited inside the Meeting House at Hancock.

It was agreed that after title had been searched, the deeds would be passed and the closing take place October 14, 1960. Searching the acreage of the Shakers' holdings was a time-consuming effort taken on by Attorney Crimmin.

The Shakers had over the years sold pieces of land to Pittsfield and Hancock neighbors nearby to straighten a line here and there. Boundaries were imaginary or nonexistent and some transactions were never recorded. Crimmin's stamina in ploughing through years of records produced some memorable material, among it the following in an early copy of *The Berkshire Eagle* headlined: "Drove Stakes *and* Departed."

> The West Pittsfield Shakers are greatly annoyed at the recklessness of sundry parties of surveyors, who have been going over their meadows laying lines for the

proposed new electric road from Troy and Albany to this city. The parties in the first place, obtained no permission to go on the land, but when they finished their work, left in the ground many short stakes which will within a short time become concealed in the grass, and therefore liable to wreck mowing machines in short order. The Shakers will remove the stakes so far as possible, and considering the uniform courtesy with which the people on the Shaker farms always meet everybody, the intruders are to be censured for the trouble they have caused.

Strange as it may seem now, the public knew little about the Shakers and many thought it impractical and useless to try to restore a Shaker village. It was necessary to do considerable proselytizing and educating of not only the public, but in some cases our families and friends. The task was made easier by a stalwart Board of Trustees, friends and former acquaintances of the Shaker family, students of American history and the local newspaper, which has loyally supported the Village. As time went on and plans were made public, many individuals who had known the Shakers came forward with personal reminiscences and important and helpful information.

The October 1960 deadline gave us time to complete the forming of a Board of Trustees and also to organize a fund-raising effort. A letter to 1,200 potential supporters in all parts of the nation was sent out September 15, 1960. It stated that arrangements had been made to acquire the important collection of Dr. and Mrs. Andrews and the Hancock Village of the Shakers. Enclosed with the letter was an eight-page booklet planned and designed by Carl Purington Rollins and printed by Connecticut Printers, Inc., under the direction of Mr. Rollins and his wife, Margaret, Chairmen of the Publications Committee, members of the Steering Committee and eventually founding trustees. Dr. Andrews, with Mr. and Mrs. Rollins, wrote the text for the small brochure which proved to be a persuasive selling piece. It was titled: *A Proposal to Save the Shaker Community at Hancock, Massachusetts: Its importance as part of the American Heritage*. On the cover was the wood-engraving of Hancock Shaker Village from John Warner Barber's *Historical Collections ... of Every Town in Massachusetts, (Worcester 1839)*. The Shaker covenant of 1795 was quoted on the first page:

> We believed we were debtors to God in relation to Each other, and all men, to improve our time and Talents in this Life, in that manner in which we might be most useful.

Eldress Emma King was sent a copy of the booklet and approved it with praise. A second booklet, titled *Realities of Restoring the Shaker Community at Hancock, Massachusetts*, was published two years later. Both are now collectors items. This was a precursor to an active publication program which will be described in detail later.

It was ironic that the last eldress at Hancock, Eldress Fannie Estabrook, died at the age of 90 on the opening day of the drive to preserve her Shaker home of some 80 years. She went to Hancock at age 10 and became a Trustee in 1919. In 1929 she was named Eldress, the last Hancock leader. She was laid to rest in the communal burial ground with her Shaker brothers and sisters, across from the Trustees' Office where she so conscientiously carried on her duties. The simple cemetery is marked with a granite monument enclosed by a wrought-iron fence. Her obituary sent to *The Berkshire Eagle* also included a four-line Shaker song composed in 1872 at Hancock and named "Our Trade." Sister Mary Dahm, one of the two remaining sisters who survived Eldress Fannie, said it characterized her life:

> *Our tools are kind and gentle words,*
> *Our shop is in the heart,*
> *And here we manufacture peace*
> *That we may such impart.*

The response to the appeal for funds was encouraging. Contributions were received not only from Pittsfield, Berkshire County and Massachusetts residents, but from 30 other states, including the 10 states where there had been 19 active Shaker settlements — and several others of brief duration.

Gifts were received in memory of people who had known the Shakers and had worked for them, or had lived near them in West Pittsfield and Richmond. It brought many endearing stories of their friendships and kindnesses. One man sent a generous contribution, saying that for years he had bought eggs from the Hancock Shakers. "They were the best and biggest eggs I've ever seen and I knew they were not charging enough for them."

The late James Madison Barker of Chicago, a senior executive with Sears, Roebuck & Co., who was born in 1888 in Barkerville, a textile-mill village about two miles east of the Shaker community, recalled what a delightful region it was for a boy to grow up in. He said that he was often sent to the Shakers by his mother to buy butter, "the best available, and when I had a nickle I would buy a little box of candied butternuts or flagroot."

Mr. Barker fished for trout in Shaker Brook above their sawmill, climbed Shaker Mountain (called Mount Sinai by the Shakers) and doted on going to the Shaker grist mill, situated on the outlet of Richmond Pond. All the hundreds of reminiscences and letters expressing interest and concern added greatly to a wider understanding of the people who had lived at Hancock, and made the effort to save the Village the more interesting.

Foundations and several individuals agreed to underwrite some restoration costs and the operating budget for two years. It was decided that the first step would be to have a survey made of the entire property, buildings and land and an evaluation of the present condition of each building pending complete restoration. Advice was sought from Charles Peterson, chief restoration architect of the National Park Service, on how to proceed with these initial steps pending the time when measured drawings could be made of all the buildings not included in the Historic American Buildings Survey (HABS) of 1932. Although Mr. Peterson was too busy to come to Hancock, he was enthusiastic about our plans and urged us to "keep at it". He also advised asking a local architect to help make an appraisal of the approximate cost of restoration.

Betram K. Little, an old friend and secretary of the Society for the Preservation of New England Antiquities, was consulted and recommended asking Roy W. Baker of Antrim, New Hampshire, a restorer of old New England structures, to make a study of the property. This was done with the approval of the Shakers, and Mr. Baker came to Hancock May 26, 1960. Now it really seemed as if we were under way. Two weeks later Attorney Morse was called and was told the Committee could offer $125,000 for the Village. This was a figure mentioned earlier, which the Steering Committee thought fair after a review of the urgent priorities as to preservation and restoration contained in Mr. Baker's detailed report.

Mr. Baker enumerated the needed emergency repairs and their costs, and projected totals for the general and long-range restoration. Each building was analyzed and assessed. There was no guesswork. It was a thorough appraisal and it gave the Committee confidence to go ahead.

At about the same time, H. Gleason Mattoon, a Pittsfield native, a professional horticulturist and editor of *Horticulture*, the nationally circulated monthly of the Massachusetts Horticultural Society, was asked for advice on how to restore the horticultural and agricultural aspects of the Village. The herb gardens obviously needed replanting, as did the apple orchard. Old trees needed to be pruned or removed, and pasture fencing needed replacing. Mr. Mattoon agreed to become consultant in these matters.

There was much work ahead and it was imperative to establish a timetable. That was the first duty of the trustees elected at a meeting at the home of Laurence R. Connor on October 19, 1960, by the members of the corporation, Shaker Community, Inc.

Several important decisions were made by the new board as a result of contributions from 243 contributors in cash and pledges amounting to $97,840 from the September appeal for support. It was the consensus that the target date for opening the Village to the public be as early in July 1961 as possible, and that certain restoration be started at once in order to have something for the public to see. Work was organized immediately to start on two key buildings, the Sisters' Shop and the 4½-story Church Family Brick Dwelling.

As soon as it was approved by the Shaker Ministry, and somewhat ahead of the passing of the deeds, the corporation, with the consent of the Shakers, took occupancy of the Trustees'

Office and engaged Philip L. Clark of Worcester, Massachusetts, to be resident superintendent of buildings and grounds beginning October 14, 1960. Philip Clark had been gardener-chauffeur with my family in Worcester from 1928 to 1957 and I had enormous faith in his abilities, integrity and resourcefulness.

Philip was known for several years as the "Shaker hermit" until his marriage in 1967 to Virginia Page. "Ginny" became the Village housekeeper — no mean job — and her care of all the buildings' interiors with little extra help is now a sobering thought. Shaker order prevailed everywhere and our visitors were constant in their praise of the exquisitely clean floors, windows and curtains. Philip and Virginia Clark retired in 1973, leaving a void hard to fill.

Many things fell into place to help meet the July deadline for opening day. An architect, Terry Hallock, had recently moved to Richmond and lived less than five miles from the Village. Mr. Hallock was recruited to undertake with Roy Baker the survey recommended by Charles Peterson and has worked from that day to this on all and any architectural projects associated with the Village. He directed the restoration of the first floor of the Dwelling in the race against time, devoting hours to supervising work on the large "gathering room" used daily by the Shaker family for religious worship, two waiting rooms, two offices, the family refectory and the Ministry dining room.

In most ventures some people are more committed than others. In the case of the trustees of Shaker Community, Inc., each and every trustee was in himself or herself a tower of strength. They worked hard themselves and also involved their friends, their neighbors and their families.

If there were some disappointments, all minor in nature, there were many delightful surprises. On one occasion when discussing the organization and style of the new corporation and its obligations, Mrs. Bruce Sanborn said she thought what we needed most and right away was "start up" money. With that she sent the treasurer $5,000 and a note: "Use this where it shows and don't mimeograph."

This delighted Winthrop M. Crane Jr., then president of Crane & Co. He was generous in providing his company's distinctive paper for all our appeals and important letters. He said, "Our paper does not take to a mimeograph machine."

The date set for opening the Village was July 1. In due course the red-letter day dawned. It was, almost to a day, 181 years after Hancock's first Shaker meeting of 1780. We were ready. Our invitations had been well received and accepted with enthusiasm, and our speakers arrived on time. Two hundred friends filled the Gathering Room of the Brick Dwelling in rows of chairs surrounding the long three-trestle Shaker work table which held its place down the middle of the room, seeming to say "I was here first."

Dr. and Mrs. Andrews greeted old friends and new ones and were greatly pleased and gratified with such an indication of interest and support for what they had worked years to bring about. They had labored daily installing their collection of choice pieces of Shaker furniture in the six rooms on the first floor which, that first year, were open to the public. In the dining room their collection of Shaker spirit drawings was on view with labels written by Dr. Andrews interpreting a religious art, not easy for the general public to understand at first view. These bright watercolors, to quote the former Village curator, June Sprigg, "represented the etherealization of an American art tradition into a uniquely Shaker form elevated from the worldly to the purer spirit of the other-worldly."

The delicate and decorative graphics were a striking contrast to the severely elegant but sparsely furnished rooms, although the Shaker-built tables, chairs and small chests in them were also works of art.

After a "Welcome to Friends of Hancock Shaker Village" as president, I introduced the first of three speakers. The Honorable Raymond S. Wilkins, Chief Justice of the Supreme Judicial Court of the Commonwealth of Massachusetts, a Village trustee, led the responses. He praised the enterprise and sounded a call for men and women in the Berkshires to join in forming a Berkshire Historical Society. Miss Margaret H. Hall, who was in the audience, must have been pleased for she had been contemplating the revival of the Berkshire Historical and Scientific Society, which had flourished from 1876, the

Philip L. Clark, resident superintendent at the Village when the Trustees assumed ownership, in 1960.

The Miller family: from the left, Mark, Lawrence K., Amy Bess, Michael, Margo and Kelton.

Centennial year, but had expired in 1913. Within a few months Miss Hall, with a generous endowment, brought the Society back to life.

The second speaker, Henry N. Flynt, president of the Heritage Foundation and restorer of Old Deerfield, telling stories certifying his reputation as a raconteur, noted that the Shakers' founder, Mother Ann Lee, arrived in New York from her native England in 1774, "a week after we raised the 'Liberty Flag' in Deerfield." Mr. Flynt pleaded that the promoters of history for popular consumption and the developers of historic projects guard against a "too easy tendency" to liven them up to attract a crowd. He urged that they strive to "prevent pollution of the stream of history."

Walter Muir Whitehill, director and librarian of the Boston Athenaeum, attacked the contemporary tendency that makes one city look like another as distinctive architecture and regional characteristics disappear all over the world, and declared that "mercifully, every community has groups who stand against the wiping out of historic buildings and individual community flavor."

These groups, he said, "cherish architecture, love good food, good drink and good conversation, and work to preserve the best of the past." With their "selective intelligence," however, he said, "they know that a great deal of the past is best forgotten."

He hit out at communities where "many city blocks look like smiles without teeth," where streets are lined with "miles of used-car lots or junkyards with the carcasses of autos." The end result, he said, is that "much of life in 1961 is monotonous, chromed, cellophaned and quite unsurprising."

Mr. Whitehill quoted from a British author, Sir John Summerson, who set up standards by which buildings should be judged for preservation and implied that the Hancock Shaker Village met such standards more than adequately.

On Hancock itself, he quoted an 1855 history of Western Massachusetts by Josiah Gilbert Holland to tell how "the Hancock Shakers on their 2,000 acres live as happily as married folks," from their appearance. And he commented that the town of Hancock named itself for John Hancock "because he was liked out here although not so well liked around Boston because he had made off with some Harvard funds."

Already by 1836, Mr. Whitehill noted, historian Holland was listing the Hancock Shakers' Round Stone Barn as a "curiosity visited by thousands." Mr. Whitehill commented that although the Shakers' celibate life "envisaged the de-population of the world, it's a great blessing that means have been found to preserve their complex of buildings here." The life of the Shaker Village cannot be recreated, he said, in quoting Summerson, but "the permanent values of this architecture is one of the chief reasons for the preservation of Hancock Shaker Village."

The Reverend Malcolm W. Eckel, rector of St. Stephen's Episcopal Church, Pittsfield, and former chaplain and assistant headmaster at the Darrow School, New Lebanon, New York, concluded the exercises with a dedicatory prayer in which he cited the faithful in the United Society of Shakers who "developed unique families of believers and carved out refuges and happy dwelling places of the spirit and bore winsome witness to the simple vocation of 'Hands to Work and Hearts to God!' We dedicate this place, the work of their hands, to their memory and to the glory of God."

It was stated in the program that "in accord with Shaker custom any who so desire are invited to speak," and several did.

The next day, following the dedication, over 400 people attended a Donors' Day reception. They viewed the rooms in the Brick Dwelling on the first floor and the kitchens and "Good Room" in the basement and walked through the first floor of the Sisters' Shop, and drank punch and champagne and ate Shaker cookies under the shelter of a cluster of spruce trees towering 75 feet, some of them 70 to 80 years old. The next day on July 3rd, the Village bell sounded at 9:30 a.m. announcing, the first day since its founding in 1790, that the Shaker Community was open to the public. The events of the weekend opening were a reminder that this was no musty re-creation of the past long gone, but a revivification of a community life that was still stirring, though faintly, until a few years ago.

We received many letters and anecdotes from those coming to the Village over the opening weekend and were grateful for the outpouring of approval and support. One in particular seems appropriate to reprint here. It was from a loyal friend, Harold P. Winchester, director of Gould Farm in Monterey:

> As I stood sipping a glass of punch Sunday afternoon (July 2) at the Donors' Day opening of Hancock Shaker Village, my mind went back in vivid recollection to July 1, 1909, just 52 years ago, when I first saw this Shaker settlement. It was another hot afternoon, but with no breeze, heavy humidity and a blazing sun. I was one of 12 members of the Albany Hi-Y walking club on its second annual two-week, 200-mile walking tour through the Berkshires.
>
> We had come over Lebanon Mountain from a short stop with the Lebanon Mountain Shakers. We found that the present Route 20 was just being paved for the first time. Only a base of egg-sized granites had been laid and we were forced to walk on them all the way over the mountain, raising blisters on our feet and covering ourselves with the gray dust. The road then was all through tall trees.
>
> I can still see us as we staggered in at the gate by the red brick dwelling house, loaded down with our red blankets, cooking utensils and grub bags. Perspiring and dusty we gratefully flopped down in the shade on the lawn just where the refreshments are being served today.
>
> As I had a letter of introduction from Eldress Anna Case of the Niskayuna Shakers, I made for the little summer house (still in use today) where I found the local eldress. She was very gracious and invited us into the kitchen in the basement at the rear of the red brick dwelling.
>
> However, as we dropped all of our cumbersome equipment on the lawn, she saw most of us were carrying revolvers in our belts. We had to drop them on the lawn, too at her request, preceded by a little pacifist speech. Those were still the days of the "Big Bang" on July Fourth and we carried them only to celebrate with blank cartridges. The twelve of us then trooped down into the basement kitchen and took turns washing off the dust in the stone-trough sink with its hand pump producing cool, refreshing water.
>
> Most of our group preferred to rest on the shady lawn rather than accept the eldress' invitation for a tour of the buildings. I remember especially the big circular stone barn. It was just at the end of the haying season. There were two hay rigs inside emptying their loads into an already stuffed hay loft. We could readily believe the claim that eight rigs with horses could unload there at one time. I also recall visiting the meeting house across the road, now gone. Busy sisters and brothers in their unique costumes seemed everywhere.

As we were about to resume our walk one of the sisters served us with a refreshing drink of cherry and strawberry juices and with some home-made cookies, thriftily reminding us they generally got ten cents for such goodies. We gladly took the hint.

As we gingerly trod on our blisters on our way to Pittsfield and Pontoosuc Lake, we spoke highly of the hospitality of the three Shaker communities we had visited that day since leaving Queechy Lake (the Canaan Shaker settlement). I have visited the Hancock Shakers many times since, but that day in 1909 and the visit last Sunday will always be the most memorable.

Visiting the Village a few days later on July 4th were Mr. and Mrs. Archibald K. Sloper of East Acres, Pontoosuc Lake, who were celebrating the anniversary of their wedding which had been performed on a nearby Shaker hillside 51 years before.

The wedding had taken place July 4, 1910, in a meadow a short distance east of the Village entrance, under a big oak tree. The Hancock Shakers, though not practicing marriage themselves, "were wonderful to us," Mr. Sloper recalled. "They sent a freezer of ice cream made with wild strawberries, a layer cake and a red Shaker cloak for the bride."

These reminiscences by Berkshire neighbors were two among many others which will appear elsewhere in this history. They belie the cranky observation of Charles Dickens when he visited Mount Lebanon and the somewhat critical impression Nathaniel Hawthorne carried away from Hancock of their celibate living arrangements and lack of privacy, stating: ". . . and one of these days, when their sect and system shall have passed away, a history of the Shakers will be a very curious book."

Personally I treasure many happy recollections of the Shakers and my friendships with them. I have enjoyed the warm and generous hospitality of Eldress Gertrude M. Soule when she was at Sabbathday Lake, Maine, and of Sister R. Mildred Barker of the same Family and now in charge of the community as trustee. Eldress Bertha Lindsay and Sister Miriam Wall at Canterbury have given loving and enthusiastic support. It was a rewarding experience to work with our revered Eldress Emma B. King and beloved Eldress Gertrude in the negotiations involving the transfer of the Hancock Community. They were exact and careful of their responsibilities to their members, but when they became convinced that our intentions were in line with their own views and that we would be faithful in discharging our obligations, their confidence and support was complete and the strength of their good wishes never diminished.

At right, the Round Stone Barn as it looked in 1960, and below, after it was restored.

RESTORATION

Antiquarians have a rule of thumb: "Better to preserve than to repair; better to repair than to restore; better to restore than to reconstruct." This maxim, clearly separating preservation, repairing and reconstructing, assigns proper values to the different techniques while justifying the judicious employment of all of them in retaining or replacing structures of the past for modern use, education and enjoyment.

Some of the 17 original buildings at Hancock — barns, shops, dwellings — were reasonably well preserved when the nonprofit educational corporation acquired them from the Shakers. Some were quickly opened as the first step in creating the public museum envisioned by the trustees. Repair began on others; protective measures were used on a few until complete restoration could be started.

At Hancock, the architectural approach started with preservation, and goes hand in hand with the basic philosophy of Shaker Community, Inc., whose trustees have permitted no plans or programs to take priority over the conservation of the Village's architectural heritage. In the following pages of this section of the history are described the steps taken to preserve and restore this unique farm-and-craft settlement whose roots go back into the late 18th and early 19th centuries. Such a project is increasingly rare in the age of computers, robots and expressways.

The bronze bell in the belfry atop the Brick Dwelling sounded briskly from 1830 to sometime in the 1950s, calling the families to meals in the Believers' dining room. Today it is heard at the beginning and end of the day, and to summon visitors to special events. It tolled slowly in a mournful rhythm the day President John F. Kennedy died, and rang out proudly when our astronauts stepped upon the moon.

Even when it is silent it seems to be heard subconsciously as a symbol of the measured order of Shaker life. As these words are written the ancient bell reverberates with history, but when its long rope is pulled it rings out a clarion call for present and future action.

From the Brick Dwelling's belfry, the highest point in the Village itself, there is a good view of most of the buildings to the south. By reentering the attic of the Dwelling and proceeding to the front of the building, the visual circuit is complete with the view of the Meeting House and six buildings on the north side of U.S. Route 20.

It is from this high perch that once again one is impressed with the ordered look of the Village: the squared-off spaces, the measured distances, the clean lines of the buildings, their well-kept, freshly painted look, their neat dooryard lawns precisely bisected with narrow roads leading to principal barns and outbuildings. Historian Walter Muir Whitehill after a visit used to say it was "an uncommonly pleasant place to be." Looking beyond the houses and shops and barns, to the north and south can be seen close by the broad fields sown to rye and oats. Beyond are the uplands which in the past supplied wood for construction and fuel and now are a self-sustaining source of income as a result of selective cutting. But this pleasant view from the topmast was not always so. In 1960 it was a seedy sight.

Although the two most spectacular restorations were, first, the Meeting House and then the Circular Stone Barn, actually the first *act* of restoration came when Philip Clark tidied up the backyard of the Trustees' House, and gave the narrow wooden bridge, which leads from the highway to the eastern entrance of the Village, a coat of white paint in 1960. At once there was a difference.

Several months before this transformation by paintbrush, architect Terry Hallock and restorer Roy Baker had done preliminary work on the Sisters' Shop, but as the Shakers were still in residence and the new corporation was not yet a legal entity, the work, other than a cursory examination, did not get under way until a few months later. Then, the Shaker Ministry and its lawyers, understanding the necessity of an exhaustive and continuous study and assessment of the work ahead, was glad to permit a team of consultants and workmen on the grounds to probe the interior of buildings to allow a complete report for the owners-to-be.

At a regular trustees' meeting preceding the beginning of restoration of the Sisters' Shop, the first project undertaken at the Village, the following statement was adopted:

> Proposed Building Restoration Policy
> for consideration by
> Hancock Shaker Community, Inc.
>
> AIMS
>
> 1. The purpose at Hancock Shaker Village is to restore the old community — its architecture, the furnishings of its buildings ... to the condition which existed here in the late eighteenth and early nineteenth centuries ... Our aim is to make the Village a project in restoration which will faithfully picture an important chapter in the religious, social and economic history of America.
> 2. To preserve the Beauty and Order that existed at that time.
> 3. To reconstruct, to Restore to Good Condition, and maintain the buildings for historical record.
> 4. To create a museum to house objects of Shaker industry in an Authentic Environment.
> 5. To make public a Shaker Village for Educational Reference.
>
> PROCEDURE
> Investigation and Documentation
>
> 1. Make Measured Drawings of the building together with a written architectural description By thorough inspection and measurement of the buildings.
>
> Will Make Possible
> a) Permanent Visual Record.
> b) Analysis of overall plan.
> c) Analysis of achitectural details, significant features, trim, colors.
> d) Analysis of structure.
>
> 2. Make an Historical Report By thorough research (former records, references, data reports, etc.)
>
> Will Make Possible
> a) A conclusion as to when building was built.
> b) When it was altered.
> c) Information as to the uses the building was put to.
> d) Events of historic interest that took place in the building.
>
> WHICH WILL DETERMINE
>
> 1. Date to which building will be restored.
> 2. Former construction and additions to be eliminated, repaired, or reconstructed.
> 3. Furnishings appropriate to the function of the building.
>
> Signed ... *Terry F. Hallock*
> RUSSELL, GIBSON & von DOHLEN
> ARCHITECTS   A.I.A.

The Meeting House

A traveler in 1817 recorded that the Hancock Meeting House was:

> ... of beautiful workmanship, painted inside a glossy Prussian blue, the steps at the door are hewn out of a solid block of white marble, and from the neatness of everything one would suppose the whole house was washed between every meeting day ... There are no fixed seats or pews in the meeting house, but only movable benches.

Elder Henry Blinn of Canterbury refers to the church at Hancock several times in his journals. In 1853 he writes: "The Meeting House is the original one and would hardly be known from those in other societies as they were all built of an exact size and one pattern," apparently referring to those Meeting Houses designed by Moses Johnson. On another visit of the same year he remarks:

> The meeting house ... remains in its primitive form. It is the cause of reflection or it sometimes produces reflection, when we see such splendid and costly edifices reared in the different societies for our personal accommodation, while the house dedicated solely to God, is left and seemingly uncared for through all the changes that may occur ... However the worship of God is not wholly confined to one particular building but the soul of the devout Believer is mindful of his duty at all times and in all places.

In August 1961, Eldress Gertrude Soule and Sister R. Mildred Barker, from Sabbathday Lake, Maine, called at Hancock for a visit. They afterwards went on to Mount Lebanon to the auction held at the Darrow School. It was learned from them that a Shaker Meeting House existed at Shirley, Massachusetts, on the site of the Industrial School for Boys, a state facility for juvenile offenders. (The state in 1908 had taken over the Shirley Shaker property for a correctional facility.) This was indeed good news, for it had been thought that the only two early Meeting Houses extant in New England were at the Shaker Communities at Canterbury, New Hampshire, and Sabbathday Lake, Maine.

The Shaker Meeting House at Shirley, Massachusetts (top), was moved in sections to Hancock, 122 miles away. Photographs at bottom show the foundation and part of the ground floor arriving at their destination.

The Meeting House or Church at Hancock had been dismantled by the Shakers in 1938. It was built there by Moses Johnson, the master builder of Shaker Meeting Houses, a Believer from Enfield, New Hampshire, who "was an expert in hewing timber and skilled in framing for building purposes." He was assigned the task of framing the Meeting House and began work on August 30, 1786, five years before the Church Family was officially organized, indicating a strong sense of commitment by the Family at Hancock to the new Society. It was completed in 1792.

On August 25, 1961, in the hope that Shirley's fine Moses Johnson building might be made available to Shaker Community, Inc., Dr. and Mrs. Andrews and Amy Bess Miller went to Shirley with Frederick J. Fahey of Dalton, superintendent of the Pittsfield Boys' Club, who was a member of the Massachusetts Youth Service Board, which administered the state school. Mr. Fahey's good offices were the persuasive element in making the Shirley Meeting House available to Hancock.

In Shirley, the Hancock delegation was told the building was not in use and was indeed scheduled to be razed, although it was in good condition.

Events developed rapidly: Mrs. Bruce Sanborn, a Lenox summer resident and a collector of Shaker furniture, heard about the structure and said that she would make it possible to have the building moved from Shirley to Hancock and re-erected on the exact site of the original one, on the north side of Route 20, beside the Ministry Shop and behind the two gates which seemed to be waiting for it.

On October 4 Mrs. Miller saw Governor John A. Volpe, who agreed that a building of such historic importance should not be destroyed. Soon after, the governor's office advised that the building would be made available to the Village "with no money involved," although a dollar was paid to the state industrial school to make it a bona fide transaction, and affidavits were filed affirming the status of the Village as a nonprofit, educational Massachusetts corporation.

Legal transactions accomplished, details were worked out with the Swampscott firm of Albert G. Doane, and soon after the new year in 1962, Mr. Doane and his crew of six started work at Shirley. He cut a 32 x 44-foot gambrel-roofed Meeting House (163 years old at that time) into nine sections, weather-protecting them with plastic sheets and numbering the clapboards as to their locations for later replacement in their original places. Then began the long 122-mile haul from Shirley to Hancock on trailer trucks.

First, the 21 original foundation stones of granite, each weighing two tons, were delivered in February to the field west of the Meeting House site, which had been cleared of four feet of snow. The stones were then set on the cellar foundation, which had been completed in October 1961.

The first section of the building arrived March 20, 1962, without incident as did the other two sections of the first floor. These three pieces were joined together and put in place on the foundation.

The fourth section had a more eventful trip. A freezing rain made visibility nil as the driver and his assistant headed for the famous Hairpin Turn of the Mohawk Trail (Route 2), which descends precipitously into North Adams.

As the curve was being maneuvered, the windshield wipers caught fire; the driver could see only by sticking his head out of the window, and then he was almost blinded by the driving sleet and fumes from the engine. His companion asked, "George, is it time to jump?" George said no, and the truck with its precious cargo made it to Hancock. Thereafter, the North Adams police met the trucks at the Hairpin Turn, giving safe escort to the remaining five sections.

The nine trips of this strange-looking cargo ended later in March, and an early spring made it possible to finish putting the total parts together, affix a new roof and reconstruct the interior.

Although the building had been cut into nine sections, it was reassembled with the loss of less than an inch to sit on its original foundation stones.

The first floor was a large open room for Sabbath meetings. From halls at the east and west ends of the building, steep stairways led to the second floor where members of the Ministry

The upper story of the Meeting House was set in place first. Afterward, the ground floor was positioned and the original clapboards replaced.

The East face of the Meeting House gets a new coat of white paint.

At the dedication of the Meeting House in 1963: from left, Abbott Lowell Cummings, Maud Weyerhaeuser Sanborn, Bruce Sanborn, the Rev. Walter D. Kring.

lived. The two eldresses had a retiring room and a sitting room on the west side and the two elders had similar quarters on the east side. In between was a joint conference room. A spacious loft occupied the entire third floor.

Meals were taken in the Ministry dining room in the Brick Dwelling House, across the highway. Later "the leadership," as they were also known, moved their sleeping quarters into the Dwelling and their former rooms were reserved as guest chambers for the visiting Ministry from other Shaker communities.

This separation of the elders from other members of the Family did not indicate a less-democratic spirit; it was simply a separation involving structure and authority. In addition to supervising the spiritual and temporal well-being of the Hancock Shakers, this Ministry had the further responsibility of overseeing the communities at Enfield, Connecticut, south of Springfield, and Tyringham, Massachusetts, which was also in Berkshire County, under what was termed a "bishopric."

Work on restoration of the Meeting House progressed on schedule. Invitations to the dedication on Thursday, May 30, 1963, announced a program of Shaker songs by the Chancel Choir of Pittsfield's South Congregational Church under the direction of Helen M. Morgan, with speakers, Abbott Lowell Cummings, then the assistant director of the Society for the Preservation of New England Antiquities, and the Reverend Walter D. Kring, minister of All Souls Unitarian Church, New York City.

Mrs. Sanborn was pleased with the arrangements and delighted with the plaque made by her grandsons. It was placed on the wall on the east entry way and read: "Dedicated to the memory of the parents of Maud Moon Weyerhaeuser Sanborn, Daniel H. Moon and Maud Mary Olin Moon."

The dedicatory program also read:

> On this Memorial Day, this structure just as importantly will always have associated with it the knowledge that Mrs. Sanborn deeply appreciated the need to recreate the church in this village, whose whole reason for being was a religious one. Her personal awareness of the need of this spiritual artifact and her sustained encouragement have

*Outside the Meeting House, Eldress Emma
B. King, Eldress Gertrude M. Soule.*

themselves contributed profoundly to the exaltation of this enterprise which so many of us here today share.

The tribute continued:

> There are times when a simple "thank you" is not enough. The Meeting House is here today because of the enthusiastic generosity of Mrs. Sanborn: both those who visit this now and those who will visit it in the future can testify in gratitude to her for its existence. But for Hancock Shaker Village, there is more to be grateful for than the addition of one historic and distinguished building. Moving and restoring this structure has been the most ambitious Village effort since this Shaker Community was acquired 2½ years ago for public preservation. The successful completion of the Meeting House project with Mrs. Sanborn's backing signals to all the Village's friends and donors an assurance that, large as our overall preservation tasks and future hopes may be, they are supported by commensurate interest and faith.

The processional for the 25-member choir was "The Humble Heart" (New Lebanon, 1822) in honor of Mrs. Sanborn, followed by "Who Will Bow and Bend Like a Willow" (Canterbury, 1843). Mr. Cummings spoke on "Master Builders of the Early Republic." Three songs were rendered. "The Happy Journey" (Watervliet, 1807) arranged by Conrad Held, for many years violinist in the Berkshire String Quartet at South Mountain in Pittsfield, and "Come Life Shaker Life" (early 19th century) and the recessional, "Simple Gifts." The assembled guests were asked to join the choir in singing the refrain of this early Shaker song:

> Come life, Shaker Life! Come life eternal!
> Shake, shake out of me all that is carnal.

The Reverend Mr. Kring spoke on "The Religious Aspects of Shaker Life." Then, in accord with Shaker custom, any who so desired were invited to speak, and several did, including Mrs. Sanborn, who thanked "all who helped me do this thing. I hope you get comfort and joy out of its use."

The program of dedication was concluded with a prayer by the Reverend Malcolm W. Eckel, rector of St. Stephen's Episcopal Church in Pittsfield, who referred to the Meeting House as "a lasting monument to a holy people and their God and our God."

A keepsake printed for the Friends of Hancock Shaker Village on the occasion of the dedication was prepared by Margaret Rollins and Dr. Andrews. It was a four-page folder of Shaker songs in facsimile with a picture on the first page from an illustration by Alice Barber Stephens for "Susanna and Sue" by Kate Douglas Wiggins. It showed Shaker brothers and sisters dancing, or marching, as it was also called. The songs were from "the manuscript hymnal written and pricked" by Mary Hazzard, New Lebanon, 1847.

Following the dedication, a dinner was given to honor Mr. and Mrs. Sanborn and their family at the residence of Mr. and Mrs. Lawrence K. Miller. Those attending were presented a keepsake: a charming rendering by Terry Hallock of the interior of the Meeting House.

In 1960, the Poultry House, above, was a sadly neglected building.

After restoration, at right, it now houses exhibition galleries and the Village's library.

The Poultry House

From the standpoint of public interest, the overland trip and relocation of the Meeting House was, up to this point, the most spectacular event in the ongoing restoration program. Of course, the critical state of the Round Stone Barn was of continuing concern and would attract national attention when the physical restoration of that unique structure was started. However, a practical matter had to be dealt with earlier: the need for larger and more efficient office space and a reception center for visitors.

The perfect solution at this juncture was the brick poultry house located in the center of Village activity directly behind the Dwelling. The fact that it was constructed of brick attests to the value placed by the Shaker family on their flocks, whose egg production provided them with revenue. Basically a sturdy structure, this building, which in addition to housing flocks of chickens was also used for birthing heifers and storing hay, was in deplorable condition.

Terry Hallock drew up plans which provided for an exhibition gallery on the east end of the building, balanced by a bookshop on the west side. Three offices, storage space, two lavatories and a small kitchen were on the second floor. The largest of the offices, which was for the director, was fitted with shelving to accommodate a growing library. The second floor also housed a conference room. The slate roof needed some replacements, but was otherwise sound.

The 11 windows on the south side of the first floor provided adequate daylight for a gallery to show the Shaker spirit drawings, although there was provision for electric lighting. A burglar alarm was also installed. The restoration work was underwritten by Mr. and Mrs. Frederick G. Beinecke, Mrs. Thomas H. Blodgett, Mr. and Mrs. Bruce Crane, Mrs. Lawrence K. Miller, Mr. Edgar Kaufman Jr. and Mrs. Edgar B. Stern.

Before rebuilding of the Poultry House could begin, there was much to be cleaned up.

Amy Bess Miller and architect Terry Hallock outside the Poultry House, after it was opened to the public.

The Round Stone Barn

The "Circular Stone Barn," built at Hancock in 1826, was from the first an object of "grand architectural curiosity... visited as a curiosity by thousands of people." This is how it was described by J. G. Holland in his "History of Western Massachusetts" (1865):

> It is 270 feet in circumference. The walls, laid in lime, are 21 feet high and between two and a half and three and a half feet thick. The mast and rafters, 53 feet long, are united at the top. The stables, on the lower floor, are 8 feet high and 12 feet long. The mangers face inward, with convenient places for throwing in hay and feed from above. The covering of the stables, which could house 52 horned cattle, is the main floor of the barn, on to which, from an offset on the south side, is a doorway for teams which can make the circuit of the floor and drive out the same way. The hay was thrown-*down* into the large area in the center. Originally the barn had a conical roof. When a fire on December 1, 1864, destroyed the superstructure, it was rebuilt with a circular loft with a louvred turret for light and air, like a small hat box on a larger one.

Nathaniel Hawthorne and Herman Melville visited Hancock on a pleasant afternoon in company with Melville's editor, Evert Duyckinck, who later described the "rambling expedition" of July 1851. As the writers traveled north from their midday picnic near Lenox, Duyckinck tells us they asked directions at a crossroad. When told they were on a road leading "to the Shakers," they determined to visit the Village.

Hawthorne had been to the sect's community at Canterbury, New Hampshire, and had accompanied Emerson on a two-day walking trip from Concord to the Shakers at Harvard, Massachusetts. There is no evidence that Melville was acquainted with the Hancock Shakers during his earlier days as a young Pittsfield schoolmaster, but on his return to the Berkshires in 1850, he had included both the New Lebanon and Hancock communities on his itinerary, visiting Hancock on July 21 of that year.

However, Hawthorne had never been to Hancock and so the outing had a destination. "We met them, the Shakers, mowing their carefully groomed fields," wrote Duyckinck, "and at the Hancock settlement met again old Father Hilliard and trod the neat quiet avenues whose stillness might be felt. Here is the great circular barn where the winter cattle feed with their heads all to a huge hay mow in the center."

Melville apparently found the structure to be of some interest as he marked a descriptive passage of it in his copy of David Dudley Field's "History of Berkshire County" (1829), a book which he had purchased shortly before his first visit to Hancock in 1850. The last sentence gives the measurements and plan of the two floors of the barn, and Field concludes: "For simply laying the stone of this building the masons were paid 500 dollars and boarded." Melville jotted an "X" next to these lines and added in a marginal note: "Amazing."

When, in 1960, the trustees took title to the property at Hancock, their greatest concern was the continuing deterioration of the Round Stone Barn. In spite of shoring up the walls, a makeshift expedient intended merely to avert the barn's total collapse, it reached such a dangerous state that in 1963 the trustees were obliged to close it to visitors.

Never since the invention of the Brownie camera had a farm building been the subject of such widespread photographic documentation. Now in its state of imminent collapse it made the pages of important newspapers. Advice from friends and well-wishers poured in. It was obvious that the future of the building could be assured only by a thorough restoration, a complex and expensive enterprise, the urgency of which was impressed upon all who viewed the widening cracks and precarious leanings of the outer walls.

As always when new approaches to old problems were contemplated, the Shakers at Canterbury were the first to know. As two events to raise money for keeping the barn from further ruin were being organized, Eldress Emma King was notified and two benefits, one in New York and the other at the Village, were explained. It brought forth the following letter to the president of the board of trustees:

August 26, 1964

Dear Amy Bess:

I received your announcement of the

44 / Hancock Shaker Village

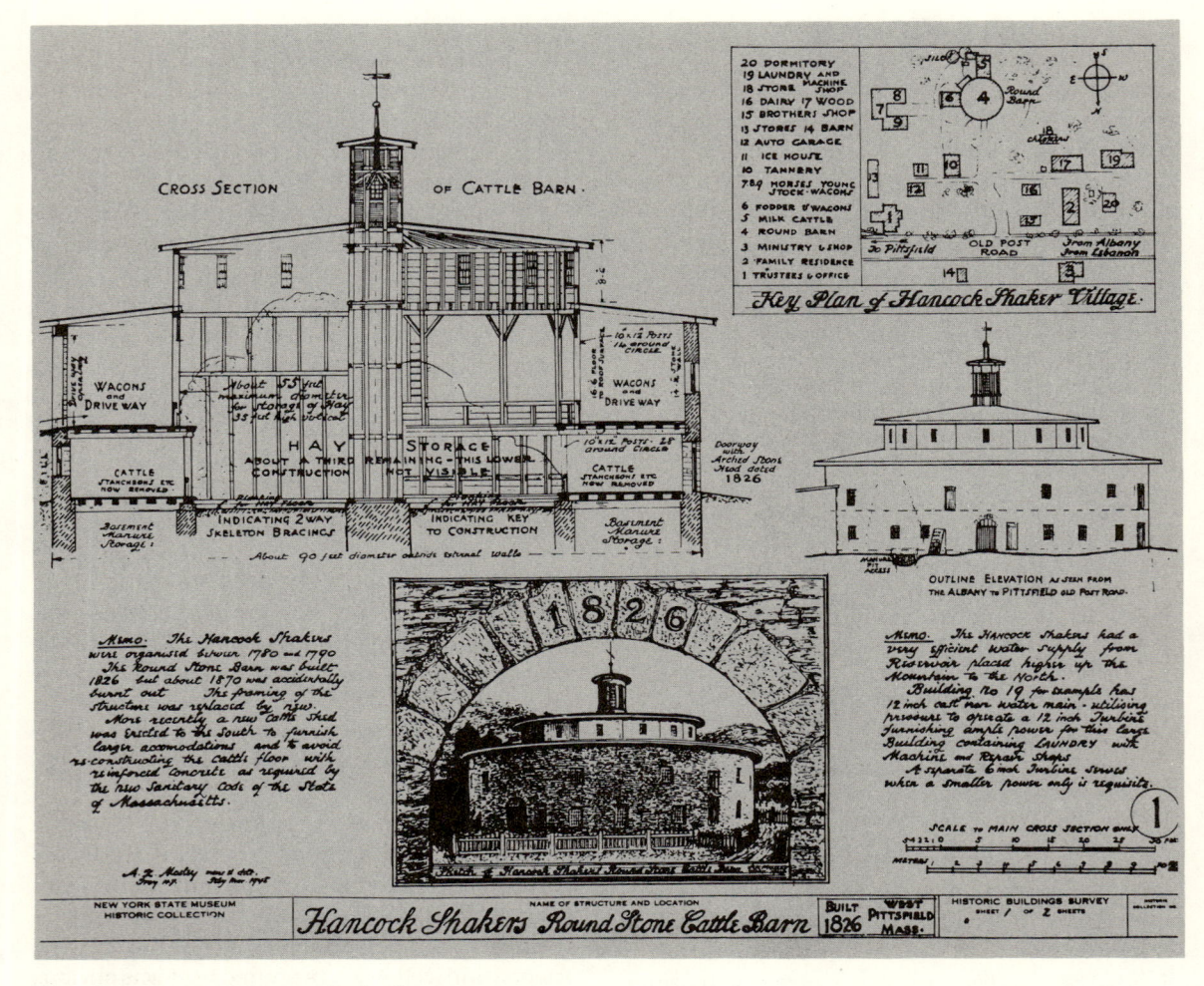

The drawings at top explain the ingenious design of the Round Stone Barn. By 1960, as the photographs show, it too was in bad shape.

Restoration / 45

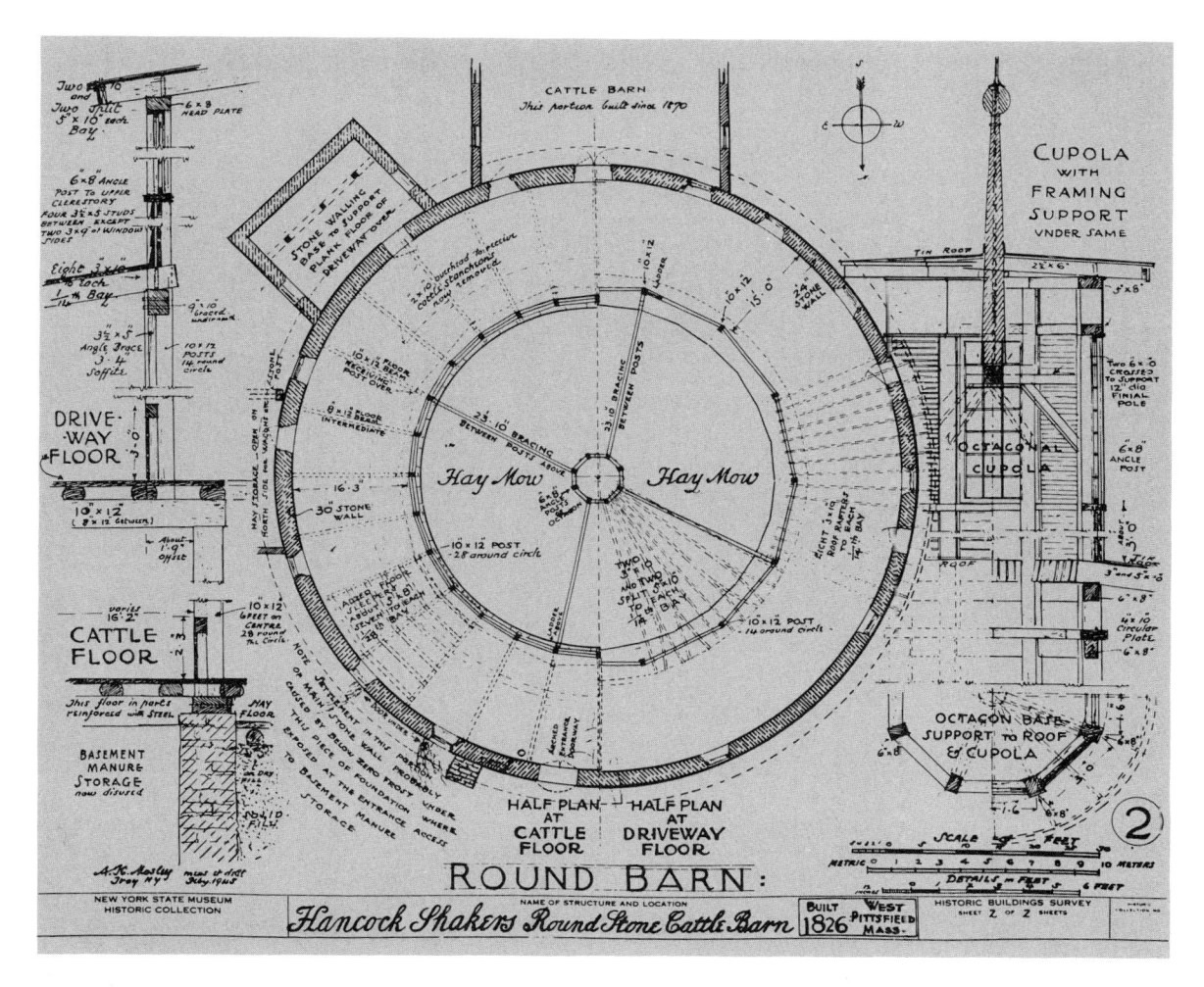

46 / Hancock Shaker Village

From left, architect Terry Hallock, Amy Bess Miller and Village curator Eugene Dodd assess the work to be done, with supervisors of the George Fuller Construction Co.

Sept. 1st meeting and thank you. It is with sincere regret that your Shaker friends realize your alarm, anxiety and deep concern over the rapid deterioration of the Shaker Round Barn. It is a historical, noteworthy landmark of the Shakers and we appreciate your efforts to restore and perpetuate its unusual architecture. Our sympathies are with you and we shall add our prayers to your devoted efforts to save the old barn and we ask God to prosper and give your united group, the wisdom, knowledge and courage for the successful restoration. God bless the special joint meeting, bless the planning and bless you all.

With sincere good wishes from your Shaker friends,

Eldress Emma B. King

Three years later it was two Berkshire neighbors who came forward and agreed to underwrite the restoration of the barn, without the necessity of a broad-based appeal. Frederick "Fritz" and Carrie Beinecke, Great Barrington summer residents, had been loyal and generous supporters of the Village from the beginning, often anonymously. Mr. Beinecke, with his interest in book collecting, had spontaneously sent books and manuscript material to the Village library, seemingly always alert to research needs.

Mrs. Beinecke had another interest in the Village. It was she who, with Mrs. Edgar B. Stern, both enthusiastic gardeners, provided funds for H. Gleason Mattoon to restore the herb garden and grounds so desperately in need of care.

The Beineckes' generosity in underwriting the Barn's restoration was joined by that of the George A. Fuller Company. The construction firm had agreed to undertake the work at cost. Work began with Village architect Terry Hallock and Fuller engineers conducting studies of the building's condition. To these studies were added the documentary evidence accumulated during the previous eight years by the Village's staff. On February 26, 1968, the Fuller Company's workmen commenced their operations, projecting a completion date of September 1. They were so confident of their ability to meet this date that the trustees designated Thursday, September 5, for the Barn's official opening, and that was the day it was held.

In the opinion of many interested friends, no other building was more worthy of attention, for it was thought to be the most appropriate existing embodiment of the philosophy of the early Shaker builders: "That is best which works best." It is one of a small number of early 19th-century American buildings which can unequivocally be termed a truly original work of art.

To most observers the Round Stone Barn, even as a relic of its former state, suggested the amplitude of self-sufficiency associated with the Shakers as farmers. Yet 30 years passed before the Hancock Shakers left scarcity behind them. From the 1780s, when the Shakers first "gathered" at Hancock, until 1810, when the community consisted of five "Families" numbering more than 145 adults, their farming barely maintained them.

A frequent lament, recorded by several Hancock Shakers who lived through these years, was the dearth of food. "We eat thin porridge three times each day," wrote one of them in 1808: "We are allowed butter only once a week, cheese almost never." The next few years, however, reversed this state of affairs completely. By 1820 there was talk of "bounteous meals" provided for a greatly increased population, nearly 300 adults distributed among six Families, and of an abundant surplus which outside purveyors were eager to buy. Their agricultural enterprises impressed a traveler in the 1820s as "the finest in the Berkshires, more prosperous now, perhaps, then any other in the County."

The Round Stone Barn, completed in 1826, made the difference. It was, as Eric Sloane said, "The Factory of the Farm." Katharine H. Annin, writing in *The Berkshire Eagle*, said it was "a symbol of excellence." It was the turning point from meager existence to prosperity. The Barn was a curiosity. It attracted attention and was considered an audacious enterprise to be undertaken by what was even in those successful years of its history, a small farm community. Its restoration 142 years later was the capstone of an effort of non-Shakers which visually and spiritually gave the friends of the restoration as much of a lift as the turn of events at Hancock had in the 1820s.

The plans for a circular barn, a highly efficient structure, never failed to amaze and intrigue beholders. The one at Hancock is believed to be the first of its type in America and was written up in many newspapers and agricultural journals. Readers from all over were fascinated by the design, especially in the Midwest, where many copies were erected. Oddly enough, few New Englanders built round barns; non-rectangular structures were more apt to be polygonal.

The latest copy of the Round Stone Barn, in enlarged form, is the antique auto museum at Heritage Plantation in Sandwich, Massachusetts. Joshua Lilly of the pharmaceutical family, seeking a suitable structure to house his extensive collection of antique automobiles, visited Hancock and found there exactly what he wanted. The Round Barn's descendant houses automotive artifacts as efficiently as the original building once housed cattle.

The barn was stripped to skeleton timbers.

Every stone was numbered, for eventual replacement in its original location. See top photograph.

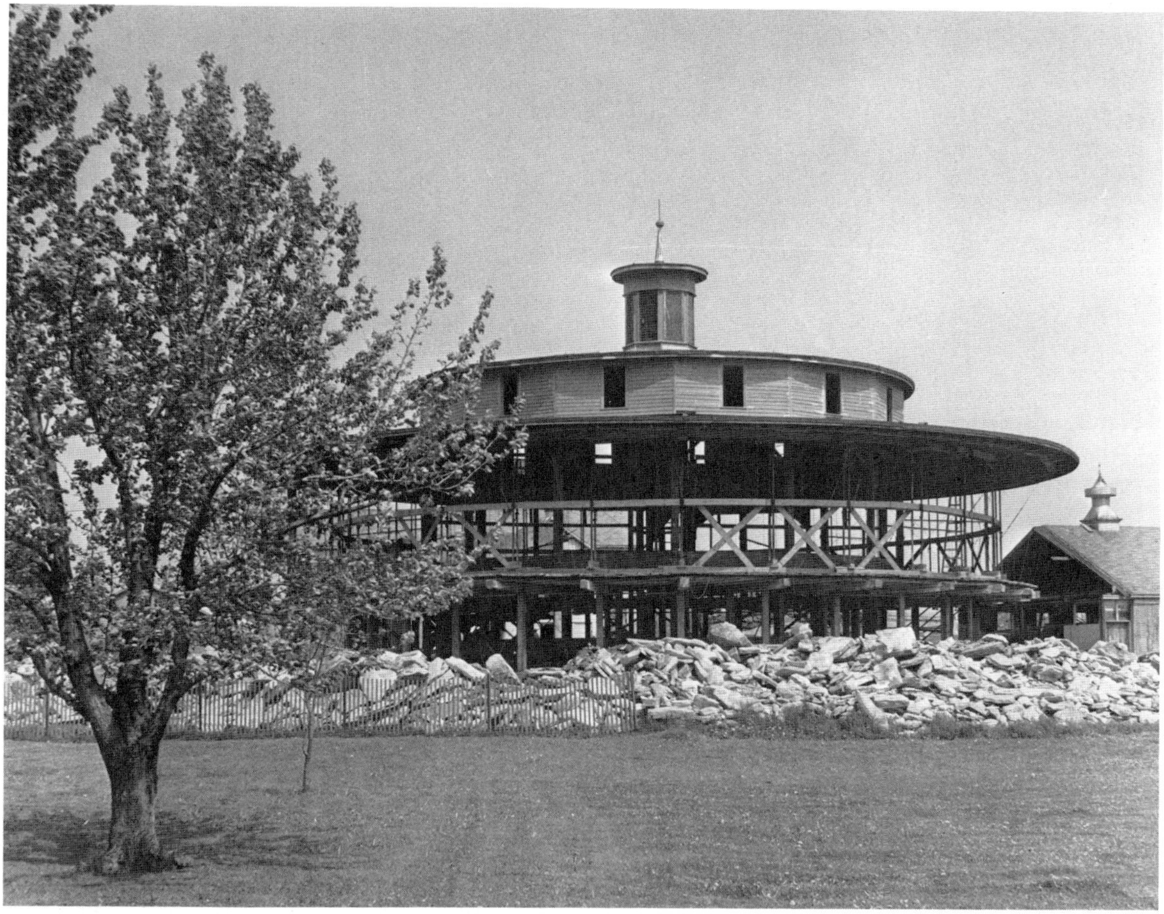

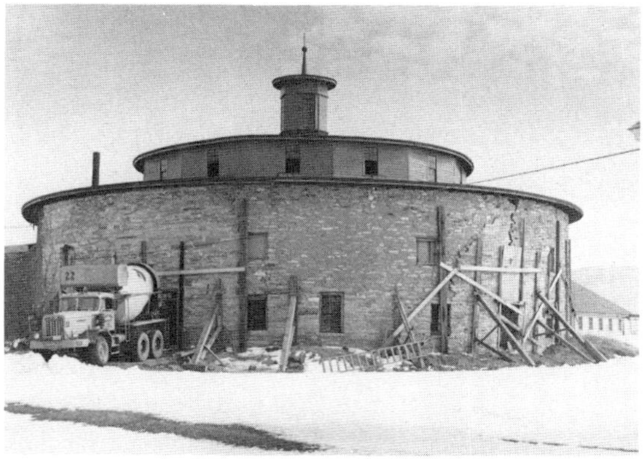

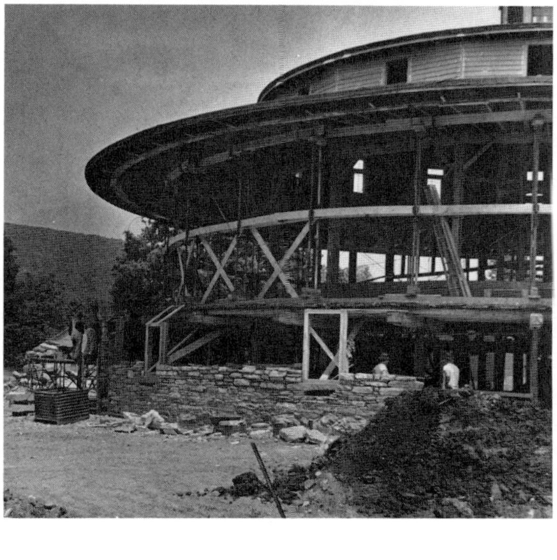

50 / Hancock Shaker Village

Shortly before they finished the job, the Fuller construction crew posed in front of the Round Stone Barn.

52 / Hancock Shaker Village

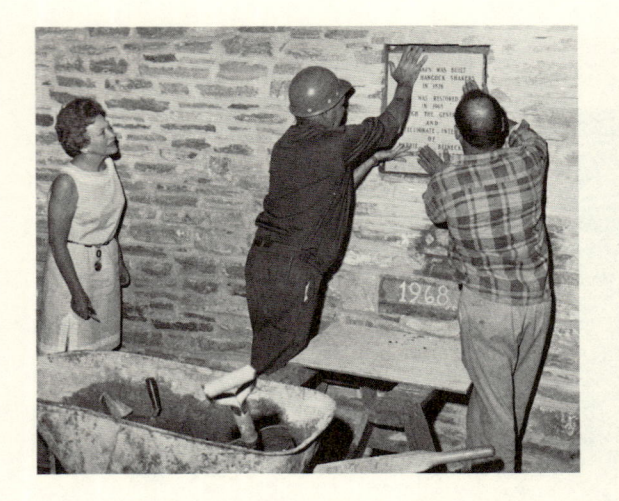

Amy Bess Miller supervises the laying of the cornerstone, above.

Eldress Gertrude M. Soule speaks at the dedication ceremony, below.

At top, going to the dedication ceremony: from left, the Rev. Malcolm Eckel, Walter Muir Whitehill, William V. Lawson, president of Fuller Construction, Amy Bess Miller and Eldress Gertrude M. Soule.

The Rev. Malcolm Eckel gives the benediction, below.

At top, Frederick W. Beinecke, Eldress Gertrude M. Soule and Amy Bess Miller, outside the barn.

Eric Sloane painted the Round Stone Barn. Chances for the painting were sold to raise money for the barn's reconstruction.

The dairy was on the ground floor of the Sisters' Dairy and Weave Shop, with the weave shop above.

Philip and Roy Baker, left, worked on the restoration of the Sisters' Dairy and Weave Shop.

The Sisters' Dairy and Weave Shop

The Sisters' Shop was restored in 1961 in time for the official opening of the Village on July 1. The importance of dairy products as part of a well-balanced diet was completely understood by the Shaker sisters; hence the dairy was an early and essential part of the Village's structure.

When Terry Hallock and Roy Baker completed their initial survey of the Village buildings, they tackled the Sisters' Shop in the fall of 1960. It was in a key spot on the interior road of the Village, close to the Brick Dwelling. Commenting on the building for *The Berkshire Eagle* in August 1961, Hallock said:

> It is difficult for visitors at the Sisters' Shop to realize the different form it once had. The building last used by the Shakers as a dairy and weave shop has an interesting history as uncovered by the late Roy Baker and his son, Philip, experts in the field of restoration. [Mr. Baker died suddenly of a heart attack March 8, 1961.]
>
> It first appeared to be a complete and original structure without a hint that it was once a building with less than half its present floor area. But to Mr. Baker's practiced eye there were unusual features about the building that could not be found in a structure built all at one time.
>
> Details, such as locations of supporting columns, spliced beams, and a basement not the same size as the building, suggested that the shop was at one time a very different size and shape. The evolution of the building was hidden beneath the wall surfaces.
>
> As clapboards, sheathing and plaster were removed in the process of restoration, the wooden frame of the building was exposed. Examination of the frame showed that the original building of 20 x 40 feet had been enlarged to 30 x 40 feet.

Hallock described the methods followed in the restoration: The building was originally one story high and that building was expanded to its present two floors and an attic not many years after the original was built in the early 1800s. A fairly recent porch on the south side was removed and two doors on the north side, one for the sisters and one for the brothers or world's people, replaced the original single door. Hallock's article concludes:

> The wooden structure is of the post and beam type of framing: 8 x 8 inch posts supporting heavy, hand-hewn timber girders and plates.
>
> Floor joists are logs with the bark still on, but leveled at the top to take the floor boards. Between the posts there are wood studs sheathed with pine boards and clapboards.
>
> Inside there are plank partitions, plastered walls and ceilings. The floors are wide pine boards. Girders and corner posts are encased in wood. The walls are white plaster with soft Shaker colors. The original colors have been duplicated.
>
> Most of the work originally was done by male members of the colony with carpentry backgrounds. It is interesting to see the varied regional backgrounds of the carpenters brought out in the individual approaches to the same problem.
>
> There are at least five different types of joists to sill plates, showing that five men did the work. The joists were patterned after popular construction methods used at that time in areas where carpenters originally plied their trade.
>
> There was extensive use of local marble on the facing of the exterior foundation and on the steps of the exterior doors.

After enlargement in the 1820s, the Sisters' Shop included a two-room weaving loft where the sisters could busy themselves while waiting for milk to arrive from the barns. Frame looms, tape looms, wool and flax wheels were all used to produce whole cloth and linen. The constant demand for these fabrics which were needed by the growing family kept the shuttles flying. In his "Guide to Hancock Shaker Village," John Ott notes: "The need for cloaks, sheets, clothing, blankets, rugs and chair tapes seemed endless, so new pieces of machinery were constantly being introduced to help with the many tasks."

At the rear of the Sisters' Shop is a dyeing frame from which hangs a large cauldron for boiling dye. Using wool from the Village's flock of sheep and flax from field crops, interpreters today prepare the material, dye it, weave it and sell it in the Village store. In doing this, the process is demonstrated to Village visitors.

On one of Eldress Emma's visits to the Village, she brought with her six glass bottles containing powders in shades of "Meeting house" blue, "Ministry" green, two shades of yellow, a red and a black. The black was used to deepen the tones of the Shaker colors. These were samples of colors to be used on the interior and exterior of buildings and on furniture. When mixed with white lead or oil they would produce "Shaker" colors. There are numerous and interesting recipes in "common-place" books as to the mixing of materials to arrive at desired and correct colors in restoration.

In repainting the building after restoration, clapboards were scraped to determine the original color. This was time-consuming as the buildings had been painted many times and for decades the practice had been to paint them all white.

It was determined in the case of the Sisters' Shop, the Brethren's Shop and the Ministry Shop to return them to their original yellow-tan. Samples were sent to the Sherwin-Williams Company and eventually a satisfactory hue was produced for these three buildings.

The shop, with the 1830 Dwelling in the background.

Mr. and Mrs. Mark Van Doren of Cornwall, Connecticut, watch a weaver at work.

The Brethren's Shop (right opposite).

The Brethren's Shop

The Brethren's Shop stands across the narrow Village road from the Sisters' Shop, east of the Brick Dwelling in the center of the Village in accordance with the Gospel order that sexes have separate work places. The two buildings are somewhat similar in structure and are painted the same color, a yellow-tan which is cheerful and catches the morning sun.

In preparing for the opening day in July 1961, the Brethren's Shop was partially restored to accommodate a few crafts. In 1973 additional restoration involving parts of the basement and refitting many of the windows was done. This building was Brother Ricardo Belden's workshop and is remembered by many for the quantity of clocks and sewing machines awaiting repair in the two front rooms on the ground floor. He also had a small living apartment on the second floor until his death in 1958, the last Shaker brother at Hancock.

A well-known Pittsfield banker tells that when he came to live in the area in 1943, he had a steeple clock, circa 1830, out of order, bearing the legend, *Connecticut*:

> Upon inquiry we learned that a certain Ricardo Belden, a brother among many sisters at the West Pittsfield or Hancock Shaker Community, was a master craftsman of wooden clock works. At an early date we visited Brother Ricardo and found him lean and spare with a bearded countenance distinguished by blue-grey steely eyes, possessing not only a comprehensive knowledge of the works of antique clocks, but also of their history. He quietly agreed to repair the clock and when we called to collect our treasure, my wife said, "Thank you very much Mr. Belden, why don't you stop by the South Street Inn [their residence] and have lunch with us." With a reflex that belied his age he countered with "When — today?" Before we could regain our poise he had disappeared into his shop.

Mr. and Mrs. Bruce Sanborn, left, and Village director Wilbur Glover, right, with a demonstrator of chair-taping.

Brother Ricardo Belden in his clock shop.

Around noon that day I was reading the newspaper while waiting for lunch in the first floor of our apartment that served as our combined living and dining space. As I turned a page a venerable but trim Model T Ford rolled up to the Inn, parked and from it, descending spryly, was Mr. Belden.

Spotting me in the window whose sill approximated the floor level, Brother Ricardo came through the fenestrated opening at a bound and promptly took my place at the table. Simultaneously as all formalities of "Welcome aboard" collapsed, Midge emerged magically from the kitchen, once described as large enough to boil an egg, but not to scramble it, with a delectable lunch for two divided three ways. For us it was the beginning of a most interesting friendship.

The Shakers had a firm belief in the order of work, and they stated: "Every man among the brothers has a trade, some of them two, even three or four trades. No one may be an idler, not even under the pretence of study, thought and contemplation. Everyone must take his part in family business; it may be farming, building, gardening, smith work, painting, everyone must follow his occupation, however high his calling or rank in the church... The Shakers believe in variety of labor for variety of occupation is a source of pleasure, and pleasure is the portion meted out by an indulgent Father to his saints."

Here today many of the crafts which were carried on by the brethren in days past are demonstrated by Village craftsmen. They might vary from year to year, but there are always several in process, and they include weaving, printing, broom-making, oval-box-making, tin-smithing, basket-making and cabinet-making.

At one corner of the shop outside stands a carriage landing: a sturdy granite slab mounted on two thick uprights and fenced in with wrought iron. There are four steps, to make it easy to climb onto the landing and into a carriage or other conveyance. The Village was most fortunate to acquire this from the Darrow School through the good offices of John Joline, when he was the headmaster. This replaced one which had been on the site but had long since disappeared.

Machine Shop & Laundry, Ministry Shop and Ice House

In May 1967, the Village received a grant from the Avalon Foundation of New York to finance restoration of three buildings: the Machine Shop and Laundry at the western end of the Village; the Ice House at the eastern end; and across the highway the Ministry Shop next to the Meeting House on the north side of the settlement.

The trustees announced that a broadly based historical approach would be followed. The underlying idea was to permit buildings of varying age and uses that changed with the years to represent the growth in Shaker thinking and progress. It became policy to restore them to their individual periods, retaining certain later Shaker additions, rather than fix an arbitrary "official" cut-off date for restoration of the Village as a whole. This policy has never been altered.

The Machine Shop building, which includes a laundry, comprises by itself something of a miniature history of the Village's architecture. As the Village grew, so did this building. Its nucleus, dating from about 1790, was augmented by at least three additions during the succeeding century. As restored, the building is in conformity with the time of its fullest development, showing Shaker technical progress from the early years of the Industrial Revolution into the 1880s.

This is a specialized building divided in half. On the east side of the first floor the brethren operated a heavy machine shop, with water-powered equipment. The sisters had their laundry and ironing rooms in the western section. An herb drying and sorting room was on the second floor.

One sister at Hancock recalled being glad to work in this building, which always smelled so clean and fresh and was cozy and warm in the winter. Sisters on laundry duty, like those in the kitchen, were rotated every few weeks to ensure that each shared equally in the work.

The laundry was for the family and did not serve the Ministry, which had its own separate Wash House for cleansing clothes and for personal bathing. This is a small brick building close by the Dwelling. It has two windows for cross ventilation. Its one door faces south and was said to provide sufficient sun to dry clothes hung on racks in mild weather. The interesting stove which heated the little Wash House is one of the earliest Shaker plate stoves. Developed along the lines of the Franklin stove, it has a wide ash shelf and hinged front face which acts as a single damper. Restoration of the Wash House involved primarily repointing the bricks, rebuilding the chimney and resetting the marble steps.

The Ministry Shop

The Ministry Shop, a two-story building, was awaiting restoration when, in 1968, a fire destroyed the north wing, which had been used as a carpentry and cabinet shop. Thanks to the prompt response of the Hancock and Pittsfield Fire Departments the blaze was mostly confined to the back of the building.

At that time the George A. Fuller Company was working on the Round Stone Barn. Since their work was progressing on schedule, several members of the work force were assigned to rebuilding the Ministry Shop. The grant from the Avalon Foundation supplemented money from the insurance company to cover the expense of rebuilding and restoring. The total cost was greatly reduced by the generosity of the Fuller Company in supplying certain necessary materials apart from those needed in the work on the Round Barn.

The important Ministry Shop, next to and east of the Meeting House, was the work area for the spiritual leaders at Hancock. Originally there were two Ministry Shops, one for the elders and another one for the eldresses. After 1850 all references to the two shops end, and it appears that in 1872-73 a new Ministry Shop was erected with both work and retiring rooms located therein, used by both sexes.

The two large rooms on the ground floor are furnished as conference and workrooms. Above are workrooms for the eldresses. Table swifts and fine furniture were turned out by the elders, and bonnets and fancy goods were made by the eldresses. The laws of the sect required even the leaders to perform some type of manual labor.

The Ice House

One of the most unusual buildings at Hancock is the Ice House, a small structure to the north of the Round Stone Barn. Dating from 1894, it was one of the last buildings to be built by the Shakers and was the subject of a short account in *The Manifesto*, the sect's monthly journal, for December of that year.

> We have long anticipated the possession of a new ice house, with modern improvements. Within the last two months it has been erected. The building is 22 x 34 feet with brick walls 18 feet high, laid in red colored mortar. One half of the lower story is finished inside with southern pine, to be for cold storage. The icehall and chamber will hold about two hundred tons of ice. The outside woodwork is painted in a light gray color, and presents quite a nice appearance. There are rooms for vegetables, fruits, meats, and many things that we may care to keep for a long or short time.

The grant from the Avalon Foundation was intended to cover the restoration of this building and provide funds for shoring up two other buildings as well, but because of the fire in the Ministry Shop, there were not sufficient funds remaining in the grant to cover the entire cost. The Kitchen Sisters, the Village's volunteer auxiliary organized in 1964, came forward and in 1970 presented $3,000 toward the Ice House restoration — money realized from the sale of their products. Thus encouraged, other friends contributed the remainder and in addition, funds to purchase a collection of tools used in ice harvesting.

One of the strengths of the Village, demonstrated again and again, is that the Village from the outset has been a communal enterprise; the underwriting of this project by the Kitchen Sisters and others is just one example of continuing group effort and generosity.

The restoration was under the direction of John Ott, then Village Curator, and James Tobin, a graduate of the Columbia School of Architecture, and at the time in the Pittsfield architectural office of Terry Hallock.

Restoration / 61

Above, the Machine Shop and Laundry, and below, the Ministry Shop.

At left, the Ice House.

62 / *Hancock Shaker Village*

The 1830 Brick Dwelling.

The Dwelling House

The central group of Believers in each Shaker society was known as the Church Family or Senior Order. On their domain was situated the Meeting House shared with the other families. At Hancock the families, named on the basis of their location in reference to the Church, were the Second, West, East, North and South families. In the heart of the Church Family's piece of land, the brick Dwelling House was completed in 1830, to accommodate a growing community of almost 100 Believers. From that time to this the 4½-story building, generously proportioned, was never crowded, even when membership was at its peak. It was then and still is the hub, the focal point of the entire Village.

Restoration of this habitation has been mentioned in connection with the dedication of the Village in 1961. At that time only seven rooms and the halls on the first floor were restored. In subsequent years the second and third floor bedrooms (called by the Shakers "retiring rooms") have been restored. Those on the west side of the house were traditionally occupied by the sisters and on the east side by the brothers. They have been restored to their original condition but not their original use.

On the second floor the rooms have been organized and furnished to show a deaconess's sewing room which houses several of the much-admired "sewing desks," a deacon's conference room, a tailor's shop, a doctor's office and a nurse shop (or infirmary) as well as three "retiring rooms," one of which is a child's bedroom with furniture to scale.

The third floor of the Dwelling is devoted to office space for the director and staff whose duties embrace the cataloging, care and display of collections, designating the educational use of the material and preparing Village publications. Research is continuous both for the use of the staff and visiting scholars. On this floor are four large rooms for the controlled storage of artifacts not on view, and material from the Mary Earle Gould collection of American woodenware, tinware, ironware and baskets, which may be seen by appointment.

The two attic floors can be viewed only on special tours. Their elegant architectural fea-

64 / *Hancock Shaker Village*

At right, the dual staircase on the second floor of the Brick Dwelling. The sisters always used the stairs to the west, and the brethren the stairs to the east.

At left, top: the elders' room, with a double desk for the trustees of the Village.

At left, below: the union meeting room.

The infirmary on the second floor.

Above, a child's room.

The flying staircase that leads to the second attic loft.

tures include a flying staircase like those built on ships, and an arrangement furnishing "borrowed light" for illuminating inside or storage rooms.

The Dwelling House early in 1960 was designated to have the basement and the two floors directly above restored for the first season. This was done almost entirely by volunteer labor. The ground floor of the 4½-story building has seven rooms, connected by wide halls intersecting in the form of a cross. These are the meeting room and two "waiting rooms" on the north and the family refectory on the south.

As in every Shaker dwelling, the rooms were laid out on a dual plan; the sisters occupied the west side of the building, the brethren the east side, each sex having its own hall and stairways. All of these rooms, plus a pantry off the dining room, have built-in butternut cupboards and drawers, rows of pegboards and paneled framing of windows, each of which had an ingenious Shaker device to open the window and secure it with screw-in pegs. At either end of the dining room on the side walls are "sliding cupboards" as the Shakers called them. To us they are dumbwaiters, originally raised and lowered by rope, hand-pulled, later electrified, to assist the sisters in transporting food from the kitchen below.

The first and second floors were in fair shape structurally at the time of the transfer of property, but the walls in the dining room had been painted pale green, the beautiful butternut trim painted white. In other rooms the same "improvements" had been made, including colorfully papered walls. Days ran into months during the fall and winter of 1960-61 and gallons of paint remover were used before the original look had been recovered. Crews of workmen, some on the payroll, but many as volunteers, worked by day and many nights.

It was truly a labor of love. The floors were in good condition and responded to scraping and refinishing. However, all the plaster ceilings needed attention. At great expense they were replaced — and what happened? The largest expanse of plaster in the main hall refused to dry on schedule and fell down four days before the public opening. It was replaced and dried by working around the clock and has held up fairly

Storage cupboards on the fourth floor.

68 / Hancock Shaker Village

From top to bottom: the basement, first, second and third floor plans of the Brick Dwelling. These were drawn by Village trustee E. Ray Pearson, who teaches at the Illinois Institute of Technology in Chicago.

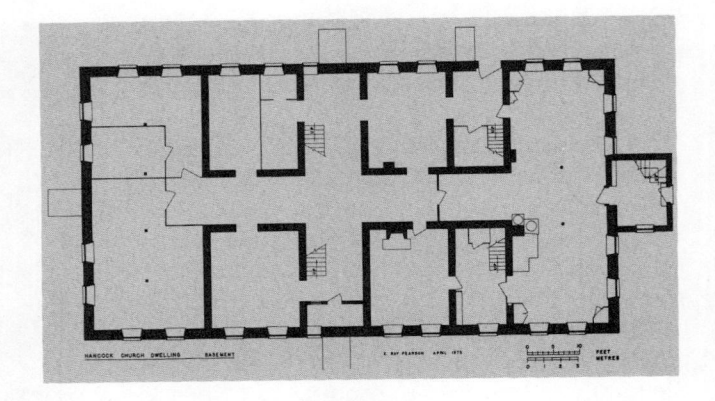

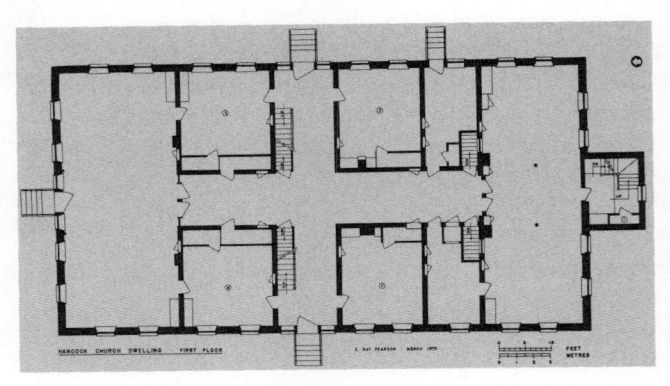

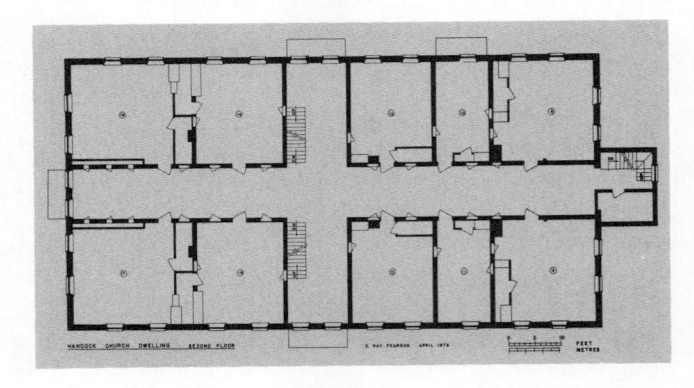

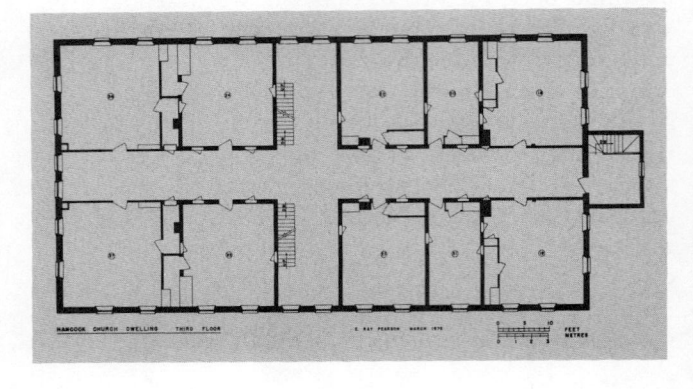

At top, the dining room; lower left, a second-floor corridor with retiring rooms: the door in the lower right-hand photo opens on a four-shelf cupboard — one of two sliding cupboards that conveyed food from the basement kitchen to the dining room, above.

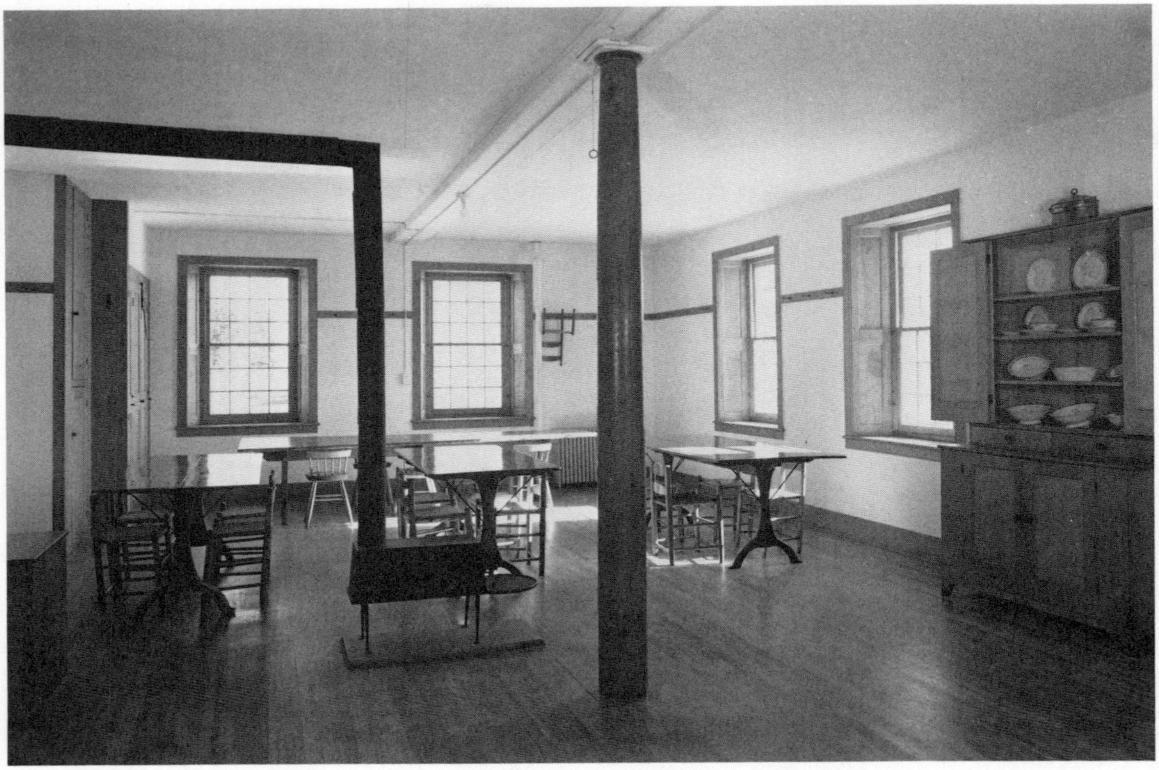

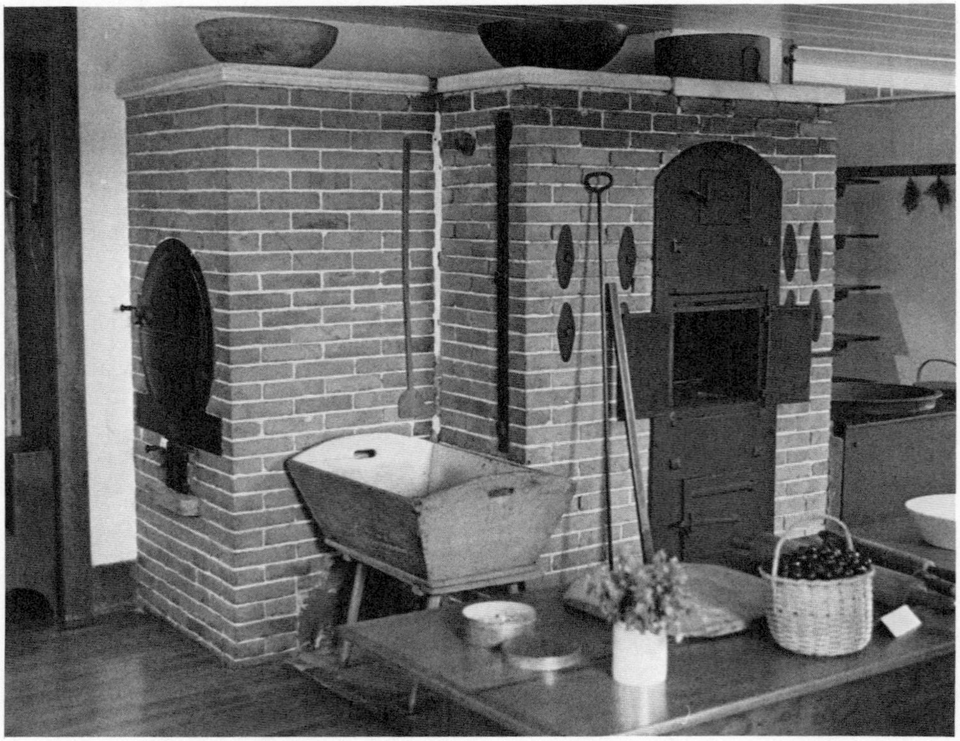

At top left, the family dining room looking east on the first floor, and below, the basement kitchen, with the pie oven at left, the bread oven in the center, and on the right the arch stove for steaming vegetables.

At top, the Ministry dining room, looking east and below, a flight of shelves used for serving dishes.

well since then, considering the vibration caused by the considerable interior foot traffic and the automobile traffic on Route 20, a few yards away.

Before the opening to the world, Sister Mary Dahm and Sister Ida Crook were asked to view the restored rooms. Sister Mary exclaimed, "Oh, what have you done to our lovely improvements?" But Sister Ida loved the clean white walls and said it was just as she remembered it.

For 21 years this large building has always claimed maintenance priority. And well it should, for today it is just as important to visitors as it was to its original inhabitants. Here the World's People's Dinners and Sunday breakfasts are held in the summer. The Good Room has its quarters in the basement.

The Brick Dwelling is described in a letter dated January 8, 1832, to the South Union (Kentucky) Ministry from Elder William Deming:

> We began laying the foundation on the 15th of April 1830 ... The work is all well done. There is none to excel it in this country. And the same can be said of the Joiner work. The stuff is very clear; Scarcely a knot can be seen in all the work... There is 100 large doors...245 cupboard doors — 369 drawers ... The drawers are faced with butternut and handsomely stained ... The Meeting Room is on the north end of the house ... The dining room is at the South end with accommodations for 80 persons ... The victuals is conveyed up into the dining room by means of two sliding cupboards ... The Ministry has a neat little dining room adjoining the large one. The cook room is very convenient: we have excellent water from a never failing spring... There is two excellent ovens made on an improved plan which will bake four different settings at one heating. Also the arch kettles are on a new plan of my own invention ... The house is accommodated with seven good stone sinks... it is finished with a bright orange color. The out doors are green. The outside of the house is painted with four coats of a beautiful red. The plastering is covered with a coat of hard finish and is a beautiful white.
>
> We have found all the materials ourselves — such as sand, lime, stone (blue limestone) etc. With all the timber except the flooring (yellow pine) ... the out expenses are about $8000. The whole

Above, a built-in iron range and the east view of the kitchen.
Right, the pie oven easily holds a dozen pies.

West view of the kitchen.

work has been performed in the space of nineteen months ... I have headed and assisted in the building of the whole house, in both the Mason and Joiner work ...

But as we have received in obedience to our good Mother Ann's words — So we expect to receive. Her precious words were this, "Your hands to work and your hearts to God, and a blessing will attend you."

We began to move in, on the 22nd of Nov. (1831). There is near 100 members well convened ...

The Dwelling House had its counterpart in every Shaker village. It reflected the warmth and habits of family life and radiated a comfortable but not extravagant style of living. It was the epitome of security.

The plan of the trustees in acquiring and restoring the Village was to make it in its physical appearance and historic functioning a *living* organization. It was anticipated that certain areas of Shaker *life* could be restored, and certain events reenacted for visitors who, like so many early travelers to the community, had been attracted to their simple communal way of life, not the least of which was the common knowledge that the Shakers, whatever their workaday regimen, were well fed. Therefore detailed restoration of the Great Kitchen was imperative. It should be authentic and useful.

Another account of the Great Kitchen in the Williams College Library tells us:

Sister Jennie leads us to the western end of the room, to a great vaulted brick oven, flanked by arched kettles, built on either side, perforated for canning 20 qts. or more apiece. Their iron fittings are hand-forged. At the left, set against the wall of the large oven, is a heating oven, with a beautifully made circular door. She [Sister Jennie] opens it easily, so perfect is the balance, and points to 4 deep shelves where 40 mince pies used to be warmed up for breakfast. Then she turns to the main oven, opening the door for us to see, explaining, "It was once lined with soapstone, but the keystone of the arch fell down years ago, so it's no good any more."

In the restoration, however, this key oven was rebuilt so the entire kitchen could be 100 per cent useful.

Sister Jennie was a "Kitchen Sister" at Hancock. She performed her duties in the "Cook Room" and dining room on a rotating basis with the other sisters. This policy of rotating duties, as mentioned previously, pertained to all those who labored at any occupation or craft in all the Shaker Societies.

Caroline B. Piercy in her "Shaker Cookbook: Not By Bread Alone," dedicates it to "The Great host of Shaker 'Kitchen Sisters' who labored to please God in preparing the viands entrusted to their hands."

So in 1964, it was only natural to follow this godly precedent. The Kitchen Sisters were reorganized and their domain was the "Good Room" on the basement level of the Brick Dwelling connected to the Great Kitchen. Originally the "Good Room," a sort of buttery, was used for storing the jams, jellies, pickles, and other preserved foods the Shaker sisters "put by" for their large family.

Present-day Kitchen Sisters, although lay cooks for the most part, are divided into two groups. The largely volunteer group manages and staffs the retail operation. The more literal Kitchen Sisters bake and put up preserved comestibles in their own kitchens and consign them to the "Good Room" for sale for which they are paid, the Village retaining one-third of the price to the buyer. The profits from the operation are designated for various restoration projects or for the purchase of needed items for museum programs.

Directing this operation for more than 10 years was Persis Wellington Fuller, a more than competent cook, whose thoughtful planning and imagination established the guidelines which are being followed so successfully today. Because of back trouble, Mrs. Fuller wore comfortable white shoes and was called by our visitors "the little Shaker lady in tennis shoes." Although no longer active on a daily basis, she keeps her eye on the "Good Room" and is regularly consulted on new procedures. Avis Drake Boice, also a Pittsfield native, made the operation of the "Good Room" possible by supplying volunteers to run it.

The Schoolhouse

When Hancock Shaker Village is spoken of as an original Shaker village dating from 1790, that is, of course, true in the broad sense. As of this writing in 1983, that statement should be qualified in order to give a precise picture of the Village today.

The Visitors' Center, or Village Office, a new building of contemporary design, will be described at the end of this chapter. In 1964, as earlier noted, the Shirley Shaker Meeting House was moved 122 miles from that eastern Shaker Village to replace an identical structure. To date, this is the only Shaker building to be moved in from elsewhere.

In 1978, an attempt was made by the trustees to purchase and move the Hancock Shaker school back to its original location in the Village. It had been sold in 1934 and moved less than an eighth of a mile away and relocated on Route 41, where it was remodeled into a dwelling house. The school had been established in 1791 on the north side of the main road almost across from the first dwelling of the early Shaker family, later to become the Trustees' Office. On April 7, 1800, the facility was set off as a separate school district by the town of Hancock and in 1817 became a public school under the jurisdiction of the town of Pittsfield, available to neighborhood children as well as children living in the Shaker Village. An 1839 Pittsfield School Committee Report states:

> The school in the Shaker district has been taught with great fidelity and system and has been a pattern of regularity, quietness, and good behavior. The improvement in all the classes has been uniform and good, but not as great as in other schools. The probable reason for this circumstance is to be found in the fact that the scholars receive only about three months in schooling a year. The boys are taught in the winter and the girls in the summer. With larger schools we might easily anticipate an amount of improvement here fully equal to any within the circle of our experience.

A few years later the curriculum was updated and became more diversified. Eldresses Anna White and Leila S. Taylor of the Mount Lebanon

The Schoolhouse, and privies.

Community, writing in their *Shakerism: Its Meaning and Message*, emphasize the conviction of Shaker leaders that a thorough education for the children in Shaker settlements was essential. This was the reason for building a schoolhouse at Hancock only nine years after the Village was established.

Mother Ann Lee, the founder of the Shaker Society, although unschooled, "recognized as does everyone else who is taught of God," according to the Mount Lebanon eldresses, "the necessity of training and developing the higher intellectual and spiritual faculties." They say her famous maxim, "Hands to work and hearts to God," has "always meant to her people work of the brains as well as the fingers." The Shakers were trained in correct habits of speech and in correct and easy composition. Shakers had to think in order to hold their own with the most acute minds of their day.

Sometime in the 1930s the schoolhouse at Hancock was closed and a large sunny southwest room on the second floor of the Brick Dwelling was substituted for it.

The trustees of the restoration felt it was essential to reestablish the schoolhouse. They offered to reproduce the little house on Route 41, adding many improvements if the owner would permit the original structure to be returned to its place in the Village, but this transaction did not take place. Failing to accomplish this important step in the restoration program, it was decided to reproduce the schoolhouse exactly from measured drawings, on its original site.

R.H. Davis of Antrim, New Hampshire, was engaged to build the school under the direction of architect Terry Hallock. It can be seen today exactly as it was remembered by Sister Olive Hayden (now Mrs. M.E. Austin) when she entered the Society in 1903 at the age of 7 and spent seven years in this school. She recalled:

> The school had 20 individual seats in four rows of five. The teacher's desk sat on a raised platform on the right with the superintendent's chair next to it and a melodeon on the opposite side. A big pot-bellied stove in the front of the room had a pipe that ran all the way to the back of the room and into the chimney. There were two doors to enter the school, the one on the east side was for the teacher to enter her washroom and where the books were stored; ours was on the opposite side with a small hall lined with pegs to hang our coats on and a large woodbox we children had to keep filled. Boys and girls each had their own privy behind the school, the boys on the left and the girls on the right.

Today the little one-room school, the two privies and a woodshed look as if they had been there since 1791 under the protecting boughs of three large catalpa trees, beside the mountain brook at its back door.

Shaker girls at school. The girls attended in summer, the boys in winter.

78 / Hancock Shaker Village

The Tan House

The Tan House, the Village's 13th restored building, derives its name from its original function as a tannery which occupied all three floors. Erected in 1835 on the site of a former cider mill, the tannery, the second one built by the Church Family, housed their leather industry, which supplied the Shaker cobblers, harness-makers and hatters. A visitor in 1846 remarked, "... we look into various places the most important of which was the Tannery which is the best establishment of the kind I have ever seen."

However, it was found more feasible by director John Ott and architect James Tobin to restore the building to its later uses for woodworking, blacksmithing and cider-making. Work began in September 1972, and was essentially completed when the Village opened its season for visitors in June 1973, well ahead of the eagerly anticipated observance of the 200th anniversary of the coming to America of the Shakers. During this period, with the skill of head mason Francis Conroy, the stone foundation, interior walls and blacksmithing forge were rebuilt with poured concrete footings for permanent stabilization.

In doing preliminary archeological research, the tannery's water cistern was uncovered at the southern end of the building. This was excavated and restored. At the north end, on the ground level, a working forge was established, and above on the loft level, a carpentry and woodworking shop.

The frame of the building had many of its deteriorated structural elements replaced, a new roof was added, and power was brought into the building through underground cable.

Also restored was the old tub turbine on the ground floor that powered the woodworking machinery above. Clifford Peck, a farmhand at the Church Family until 1952, remembers the large grinding wheel powered by a water turbine, which was on this floor. He used it often to sharpen axes, shovel blades, hoes and other farm tools. Mr. Peck assisted in the restoration of this building in 1973 and his knowledge of mechanics helped to make the water turbine and line shafts operable again.

Two principles of physics utilized by the Shakers are evidenced in this building. The first is their use of a windlass in the attic to raise heavy loads from any floor with minimal effort. The second is in the design of their cistern with sides that slope upward, smaller at the bottom than at the top, to allow for freezing ice to move upward rather than bursting the stone wall.

The large vats from the tannery operation are still buried in the floor of the Tan House beneath the Dunning-Boushort cider press of the 1880s. This functioning cider mill was moved from Great Barrington and returned to working order by John Ott and crew. It is reputed to have been one of the largest cider mills in Berkshire County, and one of the last to cease operating.

Cider was an important beverage served at Shaker meals and was carried by the brethren into the fields for their refreshment. There were apple orchards to provide fruit for the mill, and one of them was to the north of the Tan House between the Trustees' Office and the Brick Dwelling. In 1961 this orchard was replanted with varieties known to have been grown at Hancock. The trees were researched by H. Gleason Mattoon and finally located through the assistance of the Worcester (Massachusetts) Horticultural Society. Ten varieties make up the orchard, planted in honor of Edith Stern, a Hancock Shaker Village trustee. They were Golden Russet, Gravenstein, Porter, Baldwin, McIntosh, Golden Delicious, Grimes Golden, Wrights, Northern Spies and Rhode Island Greenings.

Top left: the Tan House, with the Ice House to its right.

Below, a West view of the Tan House, with the 1939 barn in the background.

The Horse Barn

One of several barns on the north side of the old highway in the original Shaker Village is the horse barn built in 1850, the only one extant today. Elder Louis Basting, who had moved to Hancock in 1887, used it for the horses and driving carriages of the Ministry and it was always referred to as Elder Louie's barn. Elder Louis was Hancock's last male member of the Ministry.

In 1974 this barn was converted into a lecture hall and gallery and fitted with a full range of audio-visual equipment. It is a sturdy and commodious building repainted its original grey and restored with its original 12 over 8 window panes. It is a good example of adaptive use. If ever a horse barn were needed it could be easily reverted to its original purpose. Shaker buildings have always been regarded as adaptable to changing needs.

Hired Men's Shop and Printing Office

The larger Shaker communities in New York State and those in Ohio and Kentucky had their own presses to print medicinal and herb labels, pamphlets, broadsides and seed catalogs, as did the smaller eastern societies at Hancock and Harvard, Massachusetts; Canterbury, New Hampshire; and Sabbathday Lake, Maine. Before 1812, Shaker publications were done by commercial printers, but in that year Josiah Tallcott Jr., a member of the Second Family at Hancock, produced the first Shaker printed work. In 1813 he reissued this work, *Millenial Praises...*, as a complete book. In 1816 a second work was printed. These two books are the earliest works printed by the eastern Shakers.

In the winter of 1976-1977 repairs were begun on a small building at the east end of the Village. It houses a printing operation on the first floor. The second floor portrays the living quarters of the hired men of the community.

In 1905 a fire had destroyed the Deacons' Shop which stood on this site, and Elder Ira Lawson ordered an unused seed shop moved from the north side of Route 20 to replace the burned buiding. The relocated structure became living quarters and shop area for some of the outside help needed to work on the farm. The use of non-Shaker males had increased as membership in the Society waned. In 1905 there were 39 members of the Church Family at Hancock and 15 hired hands.

By early spring of 1977, it was apparent that the work on this renovated building would be completed in time to open it to visitors in June. Francis Conroy and his helper, Danny Bona, masons who had worked on the restoration of the Round Stone Barn, had finished replastering the entire interior; the smooth finish left by their trowels would make any Shaker brother proud. The Village maintenance staff then applied whitewash and stain and the little building was ready.

The large print shop on the first floor was greatly enhanced by the gift of a handsome Shaker-made 10-foot case-piece of cupboards with 21 drawers, from good friends of the Village, George Abrams and Gilbert May. The Eagle Printing and Converting Corporation of Pitts-

The Hired Men's Shop and Printing Office.

field made available many pieces of equipment from their former letter-press operation, either by gift or on generous terms, and provided the expertise of their staff in setting up the equipment.

The Wilcox & Morgan press on loan to the Village from the New York Historical Association had been fully restored and Village printer Bill Root was turning out a "Keepsake" on June 25, 1977, for Village Friends. A Chandler & Price 10 x 15 job press was installed in the basement.

On the upper floor are two fairly large rooms and four smaller ones. The original dark green stain has been retained on all the built-in cupboards and drawers. The spacing of rooms and closets and the arrangement of windows make this a cheerful building.

Printers Root and Charles Seddon issue quantities of material for the Village and demonstrate this skill to visitors as they work.

Beside the Print Shop, to the west, stands the double-bay Brick Garage built in 1915 and previously described in the Introduction. This building is still awaiting some minor restoration when one or two automobiles of the proper vintage can be acquired, circa 1915-20.

The restoration of the Hired Men's House and Printing Office was made possible through the generosity and interest of the Frederick W. Beinecke Foundation and Mr. William S. Beinecke and the Eva B. Gebhard-Gourgaud Foundation.

The work of restoring this building as well as the Horse Barn and building the replica of the Schoolhouse was done by R.H. Davis and Sons, Inc., of Antrim, New Hampshire.

The Trustees' House or Office

Only by an aerial photo of the building can one understand the complexity of the problems that faced the restoration efforts for the Trustees' House and Office at the eastern edge of the Village. When Shaker Community, Inc., took over the property, the Trustees' House and Office was — and still is — a congeries of structures of different ages and styles of architecture, tacked together in a pattern that belied the simpler lines of the other buildings. No fewer than three additions had been added to the original late 18th-century frame house.

The original building on the site, erected sometime before 1790, was a small dwelling of 28 feet by 38 feet. It had been used as an office but soon proved too small for the purpose of conducting the business efforts of the Church Family, other Shaker communities and transactions with the World's People.

Sometime after 1813, the original frame structure was incorporated in a larger 2½-story dwelling which was again enlarged in 1852, this time to the south, with a peaked roof tripling the living space and making much improved accommodations and optimum ventilation. Incorporating the original house under its own roof tree with three sets of equi-spaced chimneys, its appearance was pure Shaker.

A photograph of the 1850s shows it to be exteriorly a classic Shaker design completely symmetrical with matched double entrance doors, each set facing west, and with green shuttered windows against the white clapboard siding, as described in letters.

Later in 1875 and 1876 the kitchens for the Office were moved from the basement to a new connecting wing between the main building and the adjacent woodshed with its own cupola and its 1876 bell made by the Meneely Bell Co. of West Troy, New York.

After the completion in 1831 of the Brick Dwelling to the west, and as the Family increased with more work for the trustees, enlarged office space was a major requirement. Sometime later a store was added to offer Shaker Fancy Goods and comestibles for sale to the World's People.

John Ott in his *Guide Book and History* wrote:

The Trustees' House is shown in the lower right corner of this aerial photograph of the Village.

At top: the Trustees' Office in 1853 and below, as it has looked from 1880 until the present.

The Office was remodeled in the summer of 1895, and the end result was far more than just a larger building; it was a high Victorian structure with a tower, Palladian and bay windows, bracketed porches, awnings, and interior features such as flowered wallpaper and matchboard floors. No explanation was ever recorded as to why the Shakers decided on such an ornate remodelling, but it is probable that it was an attempt to change their image. If they could show visitors and passers-by that this was a modern, up-to-date community, no longer adverse to change, perhaps more people would be encouraged to join.

This was the problem that faced architect Terry Hallock and the new trustees after he had made his investigation and measurements.

Restoration of historic places involves detailed research and those pursuing it at Hancock had the intense interest and recollections of Eldress Emma B. King. She made many visits to the Trustees' House and Office in the course of her duties as head of the Ministry as she wound down the affairs of the Family at Hancock.

During the winter of 1960 and into the summer and fall, she met on numerous occasions with those working most intimately with the project, sitting either in the Family sitting room or in the more formal "front parlor." Among other helpful gestures she made it possible for the new organization to purchase many useful appliances in the houses and barns, not Shaker-made, but used by the community and still needed. In the course of these visits she reminisced about the activities of the Family as she remembered them. If she were unsure she came back with indisputable evidence on the next visit.

It was finally decided not to take off the additions and to preserve it as it was in 1960, wallpaper and Grand Rapids furniture and all. A certain logic dictated the decision. Before the sale of the Village to a preservation group, it was the last dwelling place of the remaining Hancock sisters. In the Victorian parlor, the conditions of the sale were explained, the negotiations for the sale were conducted, and it was where the remaining sisters met their friends from the "World" and transacted their business with their hired superintendents and their business advisers from Pittsfield.

When Eldress Emma was questioned about some of the modern features of the Office, reflected in over 150 years of change, she said that always the comfort of the Family was the first consideration and she urged the new proprietors not to proceed too fast. Her admonitions have been observed and outside of necessary major maintenance, little at the Trustees' Office has been altered. The two front rooms and hall on the west side of the Trustees' House and the Fancy Goods Store have been restored and are open to visitors where they may see the business office with its imposing safe and the Victorian parlor added to the south at the turn of the century.

Since 1960 this building has been constantly inhabited, first by Philip Clark, Village superintendent, and since 1973 by John Ott, director, and his family, and now by Jerry Grant.

The original brick privy built for the Trustees' House residents, and then remodeled to house their automobile, has been returned to its prior use and is now adapted for modern restrooms.

The front parlor of the Trustees' Office, where the transfer of ownership of the Village to the present Board of Trustees took place.

The 1880 - 1910 - 1939 Barn Complex

The 1880-1910-1939 Barn Complex at the eastern end of the Village was the last group of buildings to be restored and renovated for future use. They typify the Shakers' acceptance of evolving new ideas and new equipment related to farming. In his guidebook and history, John Ott describes the physical features of these Shakers after two barn fires. They later became attached at different elevations and suited newer concepts of animal husbandry. The guide, published in 1976, concludes that "the entire complex will be restored as part of the operational farm of the museum, and will eventually house horses and cattle in the winter. Currently it contains poultry flocks and cattle."

Little did the director or the trustees envision that five years later the buildings would not house livestock, but would be a facility for making fine Shaker furniture reproductions, employing several craftsmen with a showroom, a business office and a secretary. As a matter of fact, this was not the first time since the restoration began that authentically reproduced Shaker pieces had been turned out at the Village.

The making of Shaker furniture was started at the Village in 1963 by Peter Francese, a retired contractor living in Pittsfield who made period reproduction furniture in his well-appointed home workshop as a hobby. Knowing that the trustees were planning to establish several Shaker "industries," cabinetmaking being one of them, Francese, who as a young man had been an apprentice to Anthony Guerrieri of Stockbridge, a well-known cabinetmaker, suggested that he make a start at reestablishing this particular craft. Assisted by Leo Lemieux, tables and benches of several different styles were made at the Ministry Shop from measured drawings and are today much prized by collectors.

When the Kitchen Sisters established the Good Room in the Brick Dwelling in 1964, the trustees felt that an industries program had been started, having its genesis in the activities of former brothers and sisters at Hancock. Two other shops have since been added. The Herb Shop, formerly next to the Good Room on the ground floor of the Brick Dwelling, has been relocated to the first and third floors of the Community Industries building. Here finished herbal products from the Village herb gardens and books on herbs are sold.

A third shop, established at the Trustees' Office in a room where a former Sisters' Shop had offered fancy goods for sale, is still in its original location. A variety of merchandise, including Shaker cloaks, soap and confections made from Shaker recipes, sewing notions and other fancy goods is sold here. It is called by the former name, "The Fancy Goods Store," and many visitors think the Shaker sisters are still supplying its wares. The items, all handmade, are provided by a group of volunteers who during the winter months sew and knit articles of genuine Shaker design, augmented by a smaller number of consigners.

Craftspeople on the Village summer staff for several years had made Shaker-designed articles as demonstration projects for visitors. Shaker oval boxes, oval carriers with handles, brooms, items shaped out of tin, forged-iron pieces and woven articles were marketed largely through sales to visitors in the shops. These enterprises were valuable as activities in a "living" museum and produced a certain amount of "egg money," but certainly not on a scale sufficient to perceptibly reduce a deficit.

Hence, early in 1977 a committee from the Board of Trustees was appointed to evaluate the feasibility of expanding the community industries program on a larger and more professional basis, always having in mind that all articles would be related to former Shaker industries and manufacture.

The trustees' committee sought advice on production and marketing and conferred with specialists in these fields. It also sought legal advice on the aspects of profit for a nonprofit organization. An expanded community industries program, it was reasoned, would bring a number of benefits. Available were unused buildings which when converted could be used effectively and efficiently for the production of fine-quality Shaker reproductions in wood, such as chairs, tables, beds, cupboards, case-pieces, boxes and pegboards, all in the traditional Shaker design, for sale to the public. The sale of such products made at a restored original Shaker

A woodworker demonstrating at Community Industries, housed in the restored, former horse barn.

village, it was felt, could bring in funds to sustain the operating budget of the Village and, it was hoped, provide money for necessary capital improvements. Other products, including textiles, rugs, tinware, mops, brooms, baskets and cloaks, could in time be added to the original line offered.

Several things were in favor of this plan. The rising price of Shaker-made furniture offered at auctions and antique shows had placed it beyond the reach of many who loved its simplicity and its comfort, its beauty and its character.

The committee reported that it had gone thoroughly into the advisability of expanding the industries commercially and it had also examined the 1890-1910-1939 complex of barns which it felt was adequate for the facility. It recommended such an endeavor, following professional examination and estimates of the cost of conversion by an architect. The committee further recommended that the Board consider raising a sum of money sufficient to cover the costs of restoring and adapting the barn complex for this new use. In addition, it recommended that the fund underwrite the purchase of manufacturing equipment and the payroll of the work force of artisans for a period of three years, as well as the issuing of a sales catalog and professional promotion of the products.

At its October meeting in 1978 the Board of Trustees voted to organize a capital-fund drive to carry out the recommendations of the ad hoc committee. A few months later a campaign, under the direction of the Robert J. Corcoran Company of Boston, was initiated to raise $600,000 for this purpose. The campaign, following a feasibility study and the intensive work of a large committee, was successful and the goal was over-subscribed by $200,000.

Thus, the trustees at their October 1981 meeting, having gathered at the meeting room of the Visitors' Center, inspected at the other end of the Village a substantial piece of restoration which had not been contemplated five years earlier. Signs designed from a logo prepared by Foster B. Trainor Jr., a trustee, led them to the Barns. In 1976 their director had published his guidebook to the Village and in reference to the 1880-1910-1939 Barn Complex he had written that it would eventually house livestock as part of an "operational farm of the museum." There certainly was no barn smell in the October air. There were, however, plenty of sawdust and wood shavings about.

The cows, however, had not lost out completely. They are to be housed in the dairy wing built by the Shakers in 1946, attached to the Round Stone Barn. And those cattle will have some of the choicest and certainly the most seasoned bedding of any herd around.

Visitors' Center

As restoration of the Village progressed into the 1970s and collections expanded, rooms which had housed business offices and the bookstore in the renovated Poultry House were reclaimed for museum space. Thus the need for a building of contemporary design to house these facilities and serve as a Visitors' Center became not only desirable but urgent.

Although the trustees for several years had felt the need for judicious expansion, they deliberated carefully, not wanting to hurry into a new commitment. They were reassured, however, to read what Elder Henry Clay Blinn of the Church Family at Canterbury had written in 1873 about his journey to Kentucky with visits en route to the Shaker communities south and west of his New Hampshire home. This is what he had to say about Hancock:

> In this Society everything shows a progressive spirit. The buildings are being renewed by being painted and repaired, some new ones have recently been erected. The fences are being renewed. Old buildings are being torn down. Rods upon rods of stone wall have been built and they are still at work, relaying or building.

Possibly infected by Elder Henry's "progressivism," the trustees in 1971 decided to act. The new structure, they reasoned, should not be a copy of a Shaker building, and thus it should be at some remove from the Village proper, at the western end of the herb garden. They felt a responsibility also, to provide modern restrooms and a lunch shop for visitors in an area where enlarged parking space would not encroach on the design of the Village itself.

The "New Village Office," appropriately named because the Shakers had received their visitors at the Village Office at the east end of the Village, was designed by Terry Hallock and Starbuck Smith. It was erected in 1971-72 at a cost of $65,000, with funding provided by the Weyerhaeuser, Mellon and Merrill Foundations. There it stands in what was once a hayfield, separate from but not alien to the other buildings at Hancock. Perhaps this is attributable not only to Shaker qualities that the new structure has borrowed, but also because Shaker architecture of the 1800s foreshadowed the clean vertical and horizontal lines of contemporary architecture. There is nothing deceptive about the reception center; it has the open-faced honesty of a Hancock Shaker.

The Lunch Shop opened in the new building on June 1, 1972, under the direction of Frances Persip Duval. Mrs. Duval and her father, John Persip, and other members of that respected Pittsfield family are well known to hundreds of people who have enjoyed their World's Peoples Breakfasts and Dinners at the Village.

In July 1972, a month later, the office staff and the bookstore moved into their new quarters. The building has been enlarged once since then to provide for larger restrooms, and expanded storage area and a new commercial kitchen furnished with GE appliances given by the Pittsfield General Electric Employees Fund.

Entrance to the Visitors' Center, built in 1971-72.

Gardens and Surroundings

The Tree of Life Arboretum

The Visitors' Center, however aggreable as an architectural design, had been built on a site without trees and shrubbery. To relieve the lack of greenery, to shade the parking lots and to provide windbreaks, the trustees felt that it was appropriate to establish an arboretum as had been done at Canterbury by Elder Henry Blinn. Following completion of the Center the *Tree of Life Arboretum* was established under the direction of Melva Weber of New York and Litchfield, Connecticut. Trees, rosebushes of the variety *Gallica officinalis*, and shrubs known to have been useful to the Shakers have been planted in memory and in honor of 127 people, whose names are entered in *The Tree of Life Book*.

The Shakers traditionally did not practice floriculture, but every Shaker village had its stately row of trees bordering the roadside for shade, a sugarbush, orchards of a variety of fruits, groves of nut trees, and woodlots for timber and fuel. There are still many trees at Hancock originally planted by the Shakers for shade in or near the Village. Fortunately a few large elms have survived, and a group of locusts planted years ago to harvest valuable "ironwood" for fenceposts and railway ties have seeded themselves south of the Trustees' Office at the eastern end of the Village. Near them an ancient oak stands in solitary splendor on the north side of Route 20. The last of the towering butternut trees produced vast quantities of nuts and then succumbed to old age and the west wind.

The Herb Garden and Herb Industry

Among the goals they set for themselves in the initial proposal to restore the Shaker Village, the trustees gave high priority to reviving traditional industries such as cabinetmaking, weaving, basket-making, tinsmithing, casting and forging of ironware, and — among outdoor enterprises — an herb garden patterned after the famous "physic" gardens of the Society was envisioned. The trustees felt that a revitalized herb industry could produce income to help maintain the Village, once it was established as part of the Community Industries Program.

The Church Family at Hancock planted a "kitchen garden" for the use of the Family in an area west of the Meeting House. This was kept separate from the botanical and seed gardens. A garden-seed shop, a garden-tool shed, a corn-drying house and an herb shed show on several maps or are mentioned in correspondence pertaining to the herb industry. The present "garden house" at the west end of the herb garden was in fact a summer house moved around by the Shakers from several locations at the Village and most recently moved from the rear of the Brick Dwelling where it had been since 1922 to its present location in 1961.

The impetus to revive the Herb Garden and to establish a Shaker herb industry came largely from Mrs. Frederick W. Beinecke, a summer neighbor and generous supporter of the Village from the beginning. She and Mrs. Edgar B. Stern, both enthusiastic gardeners, provided funds for H. Gleason Mattoon to restore the Herb Garden and surrounding grounds so desperately in need of care.

In 1962 Mrs. Beinecke gave a luncheon for 435 member-delegates of the Garden Club of America who were attending the organization's annual meeting in Lenox. She chose to have the event take place at the Village. Her arrangements were perfect. Tents were erected under the tall spruces on the west lawn for refreshments, another to the rear of the Brick Dwelling where a bountiful lunch was served on blue linen-covered tables, each decorated with herb-filled Shaker boxes. This was a most stylish affair located exactly in the middle of a charming old village, which then seemed to be suffering from a lack of attention and care it should have had in its declining years.

This was a good opportunity for the Village to be seen by many influential women from all parts of America, the goals of whose association are "to stimulate the knowledge and love of gardening among amateurs ... to aid in the protection of native plants and birds and to encourage civic planting." The Village was fortunate that the bushes of *Rosa gallica officinalis* planted along the fences were in bloom for these distinguished guests.

Several of the women present, delegates who had traveled a great distance, responded to the needs of the Village and contributed generously to refurbishing the property and the gardens. They had worked on conservation and restoration projects in their own zones and on National Parks committees, and were impressed with the objectives of Hancock Shaker Village.

A keepsake was given each of the guests. It was a brief history of the seed industry prepared by the Asgrow Seed Co., then of Cambridge, New York, and it stated:

> If you had been born a century and a half sooner, you might have bought your garden seed of the Shakers. It would have been good seed carefully grown, harvested at the right time, and clean. There were Shaker seed peddlers traveling from farm to farm by wagon. And Shakers seem to have originated the practice, common today, of sending fresh packets of seeds to a merchant each spring, taking back and disposing of whatever was left at the end of the season.

Given to each garden club member were three envelopes filled with seed to show how the modern seed packet changed, and the history continued: "The Mangel Wurzel (a beet from the Shaker gardens, New Lebanon, New York). The original was printed before 1861, but similar containers were used a half century later. From the standpoint of utility, carrying the seed safely and telling the gardener what to do with it, it would be hard to improve."

Rice's Seed Company. Successor to the Shaker seed business.

Shaker seed packet c. 1880.

*Suzanne de Les Derniers lecturing to class on
herb culture, 1984.*

The Dark Red Turnip Beet and Early Wonder Beet were also included in the packet in well-designed envelopes, further illustrating evolution of the modern seed package. The Asgrow discourse concluded: "We think this Asgrow Wonder Beet packet quite stylish. But we suppose it will look as dated as the Rice packet in another 75 years and only the Shaker packet will leave its age in doubt."

It was decided that until the Village undertook to raise herbs on a large enough scale for commercial purposes, an herb study garden planted with herbs grown by the Shakers could best interpret one of their most lucrative activities. Therefore, the present herb garden, patterned after one at the North Family at Mount Lebanon, contains medicinal and culinary herbs raised for sale to the "World" and for the use of physicians in making extracts and medicinal preparations.

The garden is enclosed by three rail fences painted white and planted with the Shaker rose. There are eight 90-foot rows running east and west on either side of a boardwalk and bordered with nasturiums on one side and calendulas on the other. At either end of the garden are four lateral rows of herbs. The design of the garden is not contrived, but is as near a copy as possible of one which existed until the 1940s. When it is at its best in a favorable season, say mid-August, it is a delight of scarlet beebalm, golden tansy and yarrow, the blue flowers of borage and chives and the fragrance of hyssop, basil, sage, thyme, the mints, dill and lavender. Sweet-scented geraniums, lemon verbena and rosemary are added to these in smaller clumps in the kitchen garden at the east door of the Great Kitchen of the Brick Dwelling.

William Hepworth Dixon, a visiting English editor, wrote in 1869 that he found the Shakers believing that "if you would have a lovely garden, you should live a lovely life," and in the introduction to the *Gardener's Manual*, published in 1843, the writer insists that the garden is "an index of the owner's mind." At Hancock the gardens are the products of the efforts of staff herbalists, to carry out the original plans drawn by H. Gleason Mattoon, formerly of Pittsfield.

"Orders and Regulations concerning Temporal Economy" states, "It is considered good order, to lay out, and fence all kinds of lots, fields and gardens, in a square form, where it is practicable." The large herb study garden, the kitchen garden and a garden of dye plants are neat and four-square and, best of all, productive.

It is surprising that with less than an acre of herbs under cultivation, the Village is involved in a small but profitable industry. Under Ellen Arruda's direction, assisted by Elizabeth Stell, herbs are propagated, planted, cultivated and harvested. They are then dried in a large airy room on the third floor of the Community Industries Building, packaged and sold. The results have been so satisfactory that in order to respond to the demand, plans are under way to increase the growing area.

For the past five years the Herb Shop has issued a mail-order catalog which extends the business of this particular industry throughout the fall and winter months. Products of the Village Herb Department, in addition to dried herbs, are a variety of teas, salts and peppers, mustards, vinegars, a hand lotion, a salve for burns, and a fragrant potpourri. Included in the catalog is a comprehensive list of publications on the growing, harvesting and use of herbs.

The Shaker Cemetery at Hancock

A description of the Hancock Cemetery appeared in a Pittsfield newspaper in 1896:

> There are probably 250 graves in this little yard, and they are all arranged in rows with the regularity of a chalk and plumb line, and at the head of each grave is a small plain marble slab, a little over two feet tall and a little more than a foot wide, and of those 250 slabs, less than a dozen are in any way ornamental, all of the other being practically identical as to size, shape and general appearance. On none of the marks of the graves of the Shakers is there anything concerning the life of the one whose resting place it marks, save the name, the date of death and the age... No fine gravel walks lead up to this "city of the dead" and no winding paths pass in and out among the graves; yet all is neat; and its extreme simplicity renders it attractive. In one corner by themselves are a few graves with markers a little more pretentious than those of the great majority, and they are evidently those of persons who in life were not of the Shaker faith, but in death found a resting place among them.

When the Shaker Village was deeded to Shaker Community Inc. in 1960, the Central Ministry excluded the cemetery directly across Route 20 from the Trustees' Office and made separate provisions to have it maintained. It had been previously altered in June 1943, when the uniform small tombstones were removed and a single monument was raised in their place. This was done to honor equally all the members interred there. The cemetery is enclosed with a wrought-iron fence and the inscription on the granite stone reads:

In Loving Memory
Of Members of the
SHAKER CHURCH
Who Dedicated Their Lives
To God And The Good Of Humanity
Passed To Immortality
Erected by the
West Pittsfield and Hancock Mass.
Community
In The Year
1943

In the distance beyond the cemetery to the north is Shaker Mountain, or Mount Sinai, as the Shakers called it.

Mount Sinai

All the communities in the United Society of Believers celebrated a holy feast day twice each year, one day in the spring and one in the autumn. Starting in the fresh morning hours, they walked in a solemn yet happy procession, family by family, climbing the long, steep height to a secluded spot within the communal domain.

This observance began in 1842, and at Hancock this feast was celebrated on a mountain a mile or more north of the Shaker Village, a wooded eminence which was christened Mount Sinai, sometimes called Mount Zion and known to "the World" as Shaker Mountain. In Edward D. Andrews's *The Hancock Shakers*, written in 1961, Dr. Andrews says:

> Here the Shakers cleared about half an acre of land, built a shelter, and laid out in the center a low-fenced hexagonal plot called "the Fountain." At one end of the Fountain a marble tablet was erected bearing on its inner face the inscription:

Written and Placed Here
By the command of our Lord and
Savior Jesus Christ
THE LORD'S STONE
Erected upon this Mt. Sinai, May 4th,
1843
Engraved at Hancock

A longer inscription on the outer face proclaimed that the Holy Fountain was placed there "for the healing of the Nations," and commanded that "all people who shall come to this Fountain, not to step within this enclosure, not place their hands upon this stone, while they are polluted with sin."

The Shaker feast days began early in the morning when the Believers, clad in spiritual garments and led by the Ministry, marched up the mountain two by two, passing the walnut grove and eventually arriving at the summit from where they could see, far below, their community.

It was a totally spiritual experience. Spiritual gifts were exchanged, spiritual wine was drunk, spiritual seeds were sown and after marching and singing, the ceremony culminated in a feast during which choice and exotic spiritual foods were served at an imaginary table. This pantomime ended about two in the afternoon when the marchers arrived back at the Village, now rechristened "The City of Peace."

Anna White and Leila S. Taylor, eldresses at the North Family, Mount Lebanon, New York, record "the long glad day of spiritual feasting and joy" and say that from their Holy Mount "could be seen the society of Hancock on their summit, and the two societies would shout and wave their greeting to each other, Mount calling and answering to Mount the joy of the Lord!" This could well be possible as the distance of a crow's flight between the two sites is about one mile, and in those early days, the summits of the mountains were not as heavily wooded as they are today.

In completing the restoration of the total Village and its 1,000 acres, serious thought should be given to this holy spot of the Believers. The religious life and activities of the Village would be complete if these feast grounds, where some of the most unusual services of the Society were held, could be reclaimed from the underbrush and saplings which have now closed in. Outsiders and new members of the community who witnessed the services were warned not to make fun of them for this was God's place and He was present to judge.

A few years ago an attempt was made to clear the top of the holy mountain and Eldress Gertrude Soule was informed that a group of volunteers had been working there for this purpose. She wrote back immediately saying that we should take every precaution to protect Mount Sinai from those who might not understand it, otherwise Mother Ann's blessings would leave the Village. Her point is well taken, and she has been assured that careful thought will be given to any future plans for restoring this sacred plot to its earlier use.

The Shaker Cemetery. At right, the Rev. William C. Hart and Roger W. Wellington officiated at one of the last Shaker burials in the 1950s.

COLLECTIONS

It takes good visual recall to remember the emptiness of the major buildings at the Village in 1960. As soon as Sisters Mary Dahm and Adelaide Patterson moved from the Trustees' Office, there was nothing in any of the buildings to show that a Family of 100 Shakers had lived on the land, had built up a community and existed there since 1790, sometimes in want, but more often in prosperity.

As soon as the restoration was started on the Sisters' Shop, which housed their herb, dairy and weaving industries, and as work on the first two floors of the Brick Dwelling got under way, curator Edward D. Andrews planned how the Shaker furniture and artifacts he and Mrs. Andrews had pledged to the Village would be placed and used. It was fortunate that the Dwelling and the Sisters' Shop were close together and that the Brethren's Shop, next on the list to be restored, could be partly furnished by opening day July 1, 1961, and could form an interesting tour for visitors.

Walls and ceilings were cleaned and painted, floors and the butternut door and window casings were rubbed down to an amber brown, but it took Shaker-made furniture to bring the austere rooms in the Dwelling to life. Once the chairs were hung on the pegboards, as soon as the stoves and their long pipes were installed in each of the seven first-floor rooms and when other pieces of furniture were placed, there was at once a sense of unity and "Shaker Order."

In their book, *Fruits of the Shaker Tree of Life,* subtitled *Memoirs of Fifty Years of Collecting and Research,* Dr. and Mrs. Andrews include a descriptive list of their impressive collection shown at Hancock. The preface to the catalog states:

> In any study or exhibition of the work of the American Believers, commonly called Shakers, it is essential that certain facts be kept in mind: first, that the culture was religious in foundation and perfectionist in spirit; secondly, that workmanship was a communal expression, the product of social rather than individual principles and tastes; and thirdly, that the purpose of all work done in the society was good use ...

The preface concludes with a Shaker Memorial of 1816: "Therefore our labor is to do good, in our day and generation, to all men, as far as we are able, by faithfulness and frugality in the works of our hands."

The 62 entries in the catalog cover not only the pieces Shaker Families used, but the artifacts of their crafts, industries and farming. Included also are manuscript material, periodicals, architectural drawings and, of great importance and rarity, 14 inspirational drawings.

The Andrews collection of drawings had been on view at Smith College, in Northampton, Massachusetts, in January 1961, an exhibition organized by the college's Museum of Art in conjunction with a three-day forum on all facets of Shaker life and history, called "Shaker Studies at Smith."

Besides being on view at Smith, the collection had circulated between September 1960, and May 1961, to seven academic museums in New England. The exhibition was organized at the suggestion of Dorothy Canning Miller and the publication and distribution of the catalog were made possible by the Chace Foundation, Inc. of Providence, Rhode Island. Both Miss Miller and Mrs. Malcolm Chace, Smith alumnae, were founding trustees of Hancock Shaker Village, as was Robert O. Parks, director of the Smith College Museum. Eventually, eight inspirational drawings from the Vincent Newton collection were purchased and given to the Village by Mr. and Mrs. Lawrence K. Miller.

Attendance the second year, 1962, was 8,000 paid visitors, double the previous year; also, there was much more to see. Beside the two upper floors and the Great Kitchen in the base-

Sisters' sewing room - second floor, Brick Dwelling.

ment of the Brick Dwelling, the Ministry Wash House south of the Dwelling, all on the south side of U.S. Route 20, had been restored during the winter and were open and furnished. Offices and the picture gallery were installed in the renovated and restored Poultry House which became the Reception Center.

On the north side of the highway, the first floor of the Ministry Shop next to the Meeting House was furnished and on view, and as restoration of the Meeting House progressed, there was interesting work to be followed firsthand.

In the Dwelling House, rooms on the second floor previously used for office space and storage were now restored and ready to be furnished to show a schoolroom, an infirmary or, as the Shakers called it, a "Nurse Shop," two rooms in which to exhibit clothing worn by the sisters and brothers and the tailors' counters on which they were made.

Fortunately, 50 unusually fine Shaker pieces made at the Mount Lebanon, New York, community and collected by the late Miss Mary Parsons of Lenox, and also the outstanding collection of Vincent Newton of Beverly Hills, California, who had been a summer resident of Charlemont and a friend of the Hancock Shakers for many years, became available. Mr. Newton was of great help in sharing his reminiscences with the trustees and staff.

On loan was an exhibition from the collection of Charles Sheeler, the artist, and Mrs. Sheeler of New York. It was in March of this year (1962) that Mr. Sheeler was awarded the Merit Medal of the American Academy of Arts and Letters. These 14 pieces were eventually acquired by the Village, some to be placed on the second floor of the Meeting House to furnish the five rooms occupied in 1793 by the Ministry, the two eldresses and two elders, when the church was established.

In addition to the collections already installed, word was received from Eldress Emma King at Canterbury that before long several pieces of furniture from their Sisters' Shop would be available if Hancock wanted to purchase them. Eldress Emma, a frequent visitor to Hancock, realized that much more furniture was needed to furnish all the rooms in 20 buildings. On her way to the dedication of the Emma B. King Library at the Shaker Museum in Old Chatham with Eldress Gertrude M. Soule and Sister Ida Crook, Eldress Emma urged Amy Bess Miller to visit her at Canterbury and see the furniture she had in mind.

Eventually a large moving van went to Canterbury and returned with a choice selection of 10 pieces from the Sisters' Shop, all made with exquisite care at Canterbury some 90 years before.

In 1966 the Village received 15 pieces of early Hancock-made Shaker pieces from a private collection in Rye, New York. Much of this material was incorporated in new installations, which included a Pharmacy, a Deacons' Parlor and a Brethren's Retiring Room. The following year Mary Earle Gould of Worcester, Massachusetts, gave more than 1,200 pieces from her collection of wooden, tin, wrought-iron ware, and baskets to the Village. Much of the material was Shaker-made and was integrated into the permanent collections. That portion which could not be incorporated in the public areas of the Village was installed on the third floor of the Dwelling as a sturdy collection, accessible to scholars. Also in this year friends added more than 500 items to the collections. Some of the outstanding pieces were from the notable collection of Professor and Mrs. Charles Upton of Troy, New York.

On occasion the Village has had material offered which could not be accepted for one reason or another, but during 1968, 1969 and 1970, 30 friends recognized the Village as the most fitting home for their prized Shaker artifacts. Their names are inscribed in the Donors' Book.

In 1971 Miss Fanny G. Clark, for many years assistant librarian and cataloger of the Berkshire Athenaeum, presented a diorama of two Shaker rooms in miniature, complete with scaled-down Shaker furniture made by Walfrid T. Victoreen, a well-known manual-training teacher and miniature-furniture craftsman of Pittsfield, who died in 1952. Miss Clark, who was also in charge of the genealogy and local-history collections at the Athenaeum, included in her gift funds for the construction of the diorama.

Her letter to Village President Amy Bess Miller making the donation gave a clue to her motivation for the gift: "Years ago," she wrote, "my sister and I spent a wonderful week at the 'Century of Progress' in Chicago where we were much impressed with the dioramas, both life-size and miniature. Indeed I preferred the latter, which gave vivid close-up impressions as well as wealth of detail." Additional gifts from Miss Clark included books for the library on local historical subjects.

From time to time desirable pieces of Shaker furniture and artifacts were acquired at auction through the generosity of trustees, and many other articles found their way back to Hancock, their place of origin.

The sons and daughters of the late Helen Allhusen of Verona, New Jersey, in 1971 gave the Village some 50 pieces from her collection of Shaker materials. They consisted of farm journals and diaries, day books, land-purchase records, medicine-shop journals, songbooks, and texts from the Shaker school, and meticulous records, including daily weather data, all dating from 1860 to 1940. This addition to the Village's research library also included a complete set of *The Pegboard*, the student publication of the Lebanon School (now the Darrow School).

In 1972 Professor and Mrs. Charles Upton added several dresses worn by the sisters at Watervliet, New York, to the textile and clothing collection. Donald B. Miller gave the Village an unusual large square utility box in mint condition. It was exhibited at the Visitors' Center before being added to the collection.

Mrs. J.H. Cashman of Carmel, New York, who grew up at the Mount Lebanon community where her father, Henry T. Clough, was in charge of the Medical Department, gave the Village several fine pieces of furniture and a stove as well as some important manuscripts: journals dating from 1843, extensive business correspondence of her father, medical-herb labels and account books, record books of herbs shipped to many large U.S. cities and to London, England.

The collection included the formulae of such well-known Shaker proprietaries as Seven Barks, Pain King, Norwood's Tincture and Mother Seigel's Curative Syrup and many other Shaker-made medicines in manuscript notebooks. Mr. Clough succeeded Alonzo G. Hollister as manager of the medicine business and remained 11 years. This material is unique, much of it predating Brother Alonzo's administration and spanning the prosperous years of the industry and its decline. One particularly valuable journal records the daily events of the Church Family from 1843 to 1864.

In this same year, 1972, Mr. and Mrs. Arthur A. Howard of Pittsfield and their family gave a variety of old Shaker farm implements in memory of his parents, Mr. and Mrs. Frank Howard. The gifts included a side-hill wooden beam plow, given to Frank Howard by a Mount Lebanon Shaker, Robert Valentine, shortly after Howard's Agriculture Store was founded in 1893 in Pittsfield. In addition, the gift included a two-wheeled wooden hand seeder, a hand hayrake, a heavy three-tined fork, a two-tined grub fork, a chisel, all made by the Shakers, and two planes, part of an auger and a scythe, all used by the Shakers at Mount Lebanon.

Mr. Howard said, "My father had a lot of personal affection for the Shakers and we want to share the Shaker items with other members of the community." After having seen many of the earliest plows in museums, Mr. Howard thought this plow was probably the oldest in existence in the United States. He said, "We did a barrel of business with the Shakers."

From 1973 through 1979, 158 items of furniture, baskets, tools, artifacts and manuscripts, all of museum quality, were given by 50 individuals whose names were added to *The Book of Donors*.

Several acquisitions were made possible by the trustees: an outstanding mid-19th-century watercolor sketch of Hancock Shaker Village; an extraordinary set of over 200 woodworking tools from the Canterbury Shaker Village, including beautiful Shaker-made planes marked with the initials of Eli Kidder (1783-1851), one of that community's leading woodworkers; a selection of mint-condition textiles, including hand-woven linen kerchiefs and knitted gloves, some worn by Sister Emoretta Belden (1862-1918) of Hancock; and a rare Hancock manuscript hymnal from the 1850s.

An outstanding gift was a wall clock, signed, dated and numbered "19" in 1840 by Brother Isaac N. Youngs (1793-1865) of Mount Lebanon,

Types of tall chests; at left in Meeting House, second floor, at right cupboard on chest in Dwelling.

New York (a twin clock numbered "25" was already owned by the Village) from Rear Admiral and Mrs. M.D. Matthews.

An extensive collection of early Shaker books and manuscript hymnals was received from Mrs. Harold E. Cook. Her late husband, noted Shaker music scholar and author of *Shaker Music: A Manifestation of American Folk Culture*, used many of these sources in his research. Also a handsome yellow washtub dated "1848" on the bottom, from Charles Flint.

A recent acquisition, a rare piece, is an 1851 broadside advertising a minstrel performance "for six nights only" by the Ethiopian Serenaders at Philadelphia's Chestnut Theatre. Besides such lively tunes as "Ring, Ring the Banjo" (composed expressly for the company by Stephen C. Foster) and "Camptown Races" (with a "Mr. Bones" imitation of horse racing), the handbill listed a performance of "BLACK SHAKERS," burlesques of Shaker religious dances performed in blackface that delighted worldly audiences and dismayed the Shakers themselves.

In that year at least one such group came to the attention of Hancock's Elder Grove Wright, who grumbled to Elder Grove Blanchard of Harvard, Massachusetts, "We suppose them to be another company of anti-Shakers, too lazy to work, & have taken this way to impose on the public, & to try to get a living without work."

Friends have continued to be generous in adding to the Village's collections a major gift of seven pieces from Mrs. Ronald T. Sandeberg marked the new decade of the '70s. The furniture, all from Canterbury, New Hampshire, includes a unique table-desk with drop leaf and drawers. Two side-by-side supports for the leaf allow it to be held out straight as a table or at a sloping angle as a writing surface. Another outstanding example, a small drop-leaf table with drawers is so appealing that it has been chosen for reproduction in the Village Community Industries Workshop.

In June 1981, the Village acquired all the major pieces of woodworking machinery from the late Gus Schwerdtfeger's shop near Sabbathday Lake, Maine. Gus had learned the art of oval box making from Brother Delmer Wilson so it seemed fitting that this originally Shaker-purchased machinery be put back into use in shops serving similar purposes. Jerry Grant, the Village's oval-box maker, started at once to restore the square-head plane and rigged up the lathe and bandsaw so all would run from a powered flat-belt-driven lineshaft. This has doubled production capabilities and the Village is most thankful to Alice Schwerdtfeger.

In the 1960s Shaker furniture and artifacts, which Amy Bess Miller had been assembling since she first met Dr. and Mrs. Andrews in 1938, were put on loan in various buildings at the Village as the need to furnish rooms arose. Many of the pieces were bought from the Andrewses and many had been purchased from the Shakers at Mount Lebanon and Hancock when accompanying the Andrewses on visits. Later Mrs. Miller had purchased Shaker furniture at auctions or from the Shaker Family at Canterbury. She recalled recently that it was a rare week when a dealer failed to turn up with a tempting piece. When Mr. and Mrs. Miller decided to give the collection to the Village, Robert Herron was asked to make an inventory of it and, to no one's surprise, over 200 pieces were listed.

As a separate gift, and in memory of her aunt Amy, Mrs. Frank C. Smith of Worcester, Massachusetts, Mrs. Miller gave her complete run of the first 30 years of *Antiques* magazine, collected and bound by Mrs. Smith and the next 30 years collected and bound by Mrs. Miller, to the library at the Village where they are presently being cataloged by Robert F.W. Meader, Village librarian.

In the preface to the January 1982 issue of *Antiques*, editor Wendell Garret (a trustee of Hancock Shaker Village) with pride makes a graceful fanfare in recognizing 60 years of continuous publication. he also notes that the complete set of bound copies of the magazine weighs more than 850 pounds.

Shaker furniture has been described as looking contemporary enough to have been designed in Denmark and exported to the United States. The Shakers, according to an early student of the sect, believed that their furniture was designed in heaven with the patterns sent earthward by angels. It is readily conceded by collectors that the manner in which the Shaker esthetic anticipated modern taste in design is extraordinary. The simplicity and light, airy look of the furniture makes it seem smaller and less bulky than it really is. This makes it suitable for today's lower ceilings and smaller rooms.

Thomas Merton, in an introduction to Dr. Andrews's book, *Religion in Wood*, said the "peculiar grace" of a Shaker chair could be ascribed to its maker's belief "that an angel might come and sit on it."

But if these designs were, as the Shakers sincerely believed, made in heaven, there is also evidence that the elders and deacons in charge of furniture-making and crafts were eminently practical people, striving always for perfection, abhorring the superfluous and that which would have a tendency "to feed the pride and vanity of man." Not many Shaker pieces are recognizable as the work of a particular craftsman, because of their conformity to the sect's designs. But many are obviously the work of master cabinetmakers who regularly changed jobs between field and furniture shop. Craftsmen were discouraged from signing their work (though some did discreetly) because the practice was accounted as vanity.

There is the sad account of a young brother assigned to working in the fields who asked to be transferred to the furniture shop. He was instructed to make an oval box to test his aptitude. He made several boxes, none of which was deemed acceptable by Shaker standards. Each box, the record shows, was destroyed and the young man was sent back to farming. Standards rigidly enforced led to quality workmanship.

In accepting gifts for the collections at Hancock or acquiring material by purchase, the trustees and the curators have held to the highest ideals. As Mother Ann decreed:

> Regularity is beautiful. There is great beauty in harmony. Order is creation of beauty. It is heaven's first law, the the protection of souls ... Beauty rests on utility. All beauty that has not a foundation in use, soon grows distasteful, and needs continual replacement with something new.

The trustees, the directors, curators and staff over the years since 1960 are grateful to the scores of friends who have made it possible to assemble a collection of furniture, artifacts, and farm machinery for use and display in this Shaker Village. It is not possible to name all those who have given. An object as small as a hand-knit washcloth comes to mind, as does a large chastely detailed oval box, or an exquisite sewing desk. All and each of these are prized equally, as they tell the story of the Family at Hancock.

TRUSTEES, FRIENDS, COUNCIL OF FRIENDS

The Shaker Order of Organization" was practical and explicit. It took into account all the needs of the government of the Society. As far as it is known or recorded, the organization worked.

Shaker trustees were appointed to take charge of the temporal interests and duties of the Society, the buying, the selling, the holding of deeds and so on. As has already been mentioned in the Introduction, meetings with the 20th-century eldresses who were performing the duties of the trustees, were pleasant, informative and always helpful.

When forming the Board of Trustees of the new corporation, it was the unanimous feeling that there should be a Shaker on the Board "in order that we be not removed completely from the Shaker movement and its tradition." Eldress Emma B. King of the Canterbury Society was asked to be honorary trustee and upon her death in 1966, Eldress Gertrude M. Soule of the Sabbathday Lake Shakers was asked to succeed her.

Their letters, frequent visits to the Village, their warmth of feeling for those working to preserve Hancock and their prayers "that God's tender love would always be over those with the responsibility of the work," were heartening.

Eldress Emma in accepting the invitation to serve on the Board wrote that she was pleased and would do all she could to help the project "prosper." When the president of the Board wrote her once that she had a tendency to work too fast, Eldress Emma wrote back, "At my age I wish I had worked faster. It is good you work fast, there is much to be done and you have good helpers." If she had misgivings, she did not permit them to discourage the workers.

When Eldress Gertrude was asked to succeed Eldress Emma on the Board she replied, "Your most kind invitation to be an Honorary Trustee brought a great surprise to me. I do not feel worthy of such a great honor. I will accept the invitation you and your group of Trustees have sincerely extended. I feel honored to be chosen and also to be chosen in beloved Eldress Emma's chosen place." The guidance of these two extraordinary Believers has been a major factor in the success of the restoration of Hancock Shaker Village.

Of the original 25 founding trustees, 14 are still on the Board. Five of the first trustees died, but three of their widows were elected. Four of the original trustees resigned two years after the founding of the Board and when other resignations were sent in, it was because relocation made the distance for regular attendance at meetings difficult, or because of ill health. Therefore, there has been continuity of direction and interest.

The concern and involvement of the trustees has been and continues to be the great strength of this organization. Whether there was a meeting scheduled or not, many trustees would come to the Village just to absorb the atmosphere and often to show it for the first time to their friends.

On one such occasion in 1960, Edith Stern, an early trustee who was a Lenox summer resident, walked around the Round Stone Barn, past the Poultry House to the Machine Shop and Laundry and on to the Brick Dwelling, taking in the spectacle of benign neglect and the ravages of time. After a thoughtful silence, she said: "Brick by brick is the way you build a wall. You don't get discouraged. You just keep at it and I will contribute to the running costs for two years ... just take one brick at a time."

Some years later after receiving an encouraging report from the treasurer, she responded: "I like a balanced budget." The report had also included a record of the approximate cost of restoration from 1960 to 1970 which topped $2 million. Her reply to this was: "To think that 10 years ago some people said we would never fly. I knew we would."

Hancock Shaker Village Trustees, October, 1982.
First row, left to right: Robert G. Newman, Mrs. Foster B. Trainer, Jr., Mrs. Henry A. Murray, Mrs. Ludwig G. Lederer, Eldress Gertrude M. Soule, Mrs. Lawrence K. Miller, Mrs. Malcolm G. Chace, Jr., Mrs. Frank M. Faucett, Samuel Boxer. Second row, left to right: Foster B. Trainer, Jr., Frederick L. Rath, Jr., Robert L. Raley, C. Frederick Rudolph, Frederick G. Crane, Jr., Lawrence K. Miller, John H. Ott, William Henry Harrison IV, Richard S. Jackson, Jr., Stuart C. Henry, John W. Calkins, David W. Murphy, Terry Hallock.

Another trustee, Massachusetts Chief Justice Raymond S. Wilkins, whose mother had collected Shaker furniture, wrote after attending a meeting at Hancock: "I have listened to my mother talk about the Shakers and Miss Sears' interests at Harvard for years and I thought I knew quite a bit about the Shakers, but nothing compared to what I have learned since attending meetings at Hancock and what, no doubt, is still in store for me."

He would have liked what a Shaker schoolboy scrawled on the wall of a carriage shed at Mount Lebanon in 1880:

> THE WHOLE WORLD IS A PUBLIC SCHOOL
> AND OUR HOME IS BUT A CLASSROOM

Eldress Bertha Lindsay, although not a trustee, came to some meetings with Eldress Gertrude and Sister Miriam Wall. After one visit and a meeting of the Board, Eldress Bertha wrote:

> I could not help think of the consecrated souls who had lived and worked there for so many years, while walking through the various homes. The barn is magnificent, in fact, everything is so beautifully done. I enjoyed the wonderful lunch and can appreciate the careful preparation that went into it... I loved it all. It made me feel so proud that I was a Shaker sister, a small part of a great heritage. I ask God's blessing on you and your endeavors.

After another meeting she wrote: "I loved every minute of my visit, for I received inspiration to continue our work of restoration." Nine years later at the redoubtable age of 85 she was still very much involved in restoration at the Canterbury Shaker Village.

In an area where the spring season is as tardy and brief as in the Berkshires, the trustees might have chosen some time other than March for their annual meetings. The bylaws stipulate that the meeting shall be held not later than 90 days after the end of the Village's fiscal year, which is the calendar year. Professor S. Lane Faison, a founding trustee with a good attendance record, recalls how hard it was to keep warm at the luncheons which followed the early meetings in the Brethren's Dining Room of the Brick Dwelling. He says: "We wore complete outer garments, overcoats, sweaters, mufflers, etc., and should have eaten with our gloves on."

Another trustee remembers that a fellow member sitting next to him leaned over so far trying to get just a little nearer the comforting Shaker stove that he fell over backwards off the Shaker bench.

The president, Amy Bess Miller, often began meetings with a bit of Shaker lore, newly uncovered, or letters from schoolchildren and their revealing reactions after having toured the Village. At one meeting a letter was read from a convict in a California penitentiary asking to have sent to him some more of the Hancock herb mix. He complained that the first shipment from the Village had been confiscated because it contained marijuana. There was no record of such a shipment to California, nor was this a put-on as the letter was marked "cleared" by some prison authority. It remains a mystery.

Knowing that the trustees enjoyed authentic stories about the Shakers, Frederick D. Rettalick of Pittsfield put the following on tape in 1964 to be transcribed and read at the next meeting:

> My father was superintendent of the Shaker farm at Hancock and I grew up in a Shaker house provided for us on the north side of what is now Route 20. The house no longer stands, but it was half way up the mountain [the West Family]. I did lots of chores working with my father and when I was old enough to go to high school the Shakers gave me a fine horse and a cart to drive into Pittsfield, fall and spring. In the winter they let me take one of their very nice sleighs and needless to say I felt very grand.
>
> One winter day coming back to the Village I was passed by an elder from the Mount Lebanon community. He looked pretty smug as he overtook me and for some reason I decided to race him. My horse was better and faster than his and on the flat just west of the Second Family where the Village first comes into view I got a good distance ahead of him, but he wouldn't give in. As I came in view of the Trustees' Office I saw old Louis Bastings waiting for me as he usually did. I didn't pull in and I certainly won the race. The Trustee was very fierce looking and he told me to put my horse away and come into his office. When I returned he looked stern and didn't ask me to sit down. "Frederick," he said, "thee knows we don't

approve of racing." There was a long pause, "But," he said, "I am glad thee won."

Mother Ann Lee once said: "Do all your work as though you had a thousand years to live, and as you would if you knew you must die tomorrow." It is a proverb worth recalling as the Shaker settlement at Hancock enters its third decade in public service. For the Believers the aphorism was relevant. Firm in their religious belief, secure in their habitation, surrounded by fertile fields, and strong in their commitment to work, fulfillment of this precept was not beyond reasonable expectation. On this 25th anniversary year, the question could be asked: Has a disparate group of World's People measured up to this marching order?

By large consensus, the answer, in Shaker parlance, would be "Yea." Many people and groups of people have helped to make this answer affirmative. Early benefactors, who put their money on a dream, inspired others who believed in the renewal of the Shaker spirit and its meaning in today's world. A sturdy band of trustees who have assumed the responsibility step by step in the preservation and restoration of Hancock have inspired over a thousand others to become Friends of Hancock Shaker Village. Each group has given generously of its time and resources.

At a recent meeting the trustees were asked to discuss new ways and means of support for the operating budget, in order to avoid a substantial deficit. Having a deficit was anticipated because, as with many organizations, inflation was taking its toll. Also, a federal grant to help cover operating costs would not be forthcoming.

Many ideas were discussed as to ways of generating more income. Some were excellent, original and good business procedures. The meeting went longer than usual and was about to be adjourned when one trustee asked to speak. It was Dr. Beatrice B. Berle and she said:

> While I find the discussion on museums as business enterprises both interesting and important, we must not lose sight of the purpose for which museums were created. The profit motive, sacrificing educational and aesthetic values, surely cannot be paramount. The need to make ends meet calls for an appraisal and definition of the values we live by in this restored Shaker community. The peculiar genius of the directors of this enterprise, I believe, consists in developing in staff members, both permanent, summer and volunteers, a sense of *"Hands to Work and Hearts to God"* which they can translate to their own lives long after they have left the Village. In other words, we are not just preserving and exhibiting objects but educating people in the deepest sense of that word. Educate and lead forward.

Those who responded to the first appeal letter mailed September 10, 1960, were made Friends of Hancock Shaker Village. They were the first to know that a group had been formed to buy the Shaker Village and restore it. They were also told that $250,000 was needed for the project, an original, complete and integrated community dating to the founding days of our Republic. They were also told that because of this uniqueness, there had been considerable interest shown by foundations and that foundations were more readily impelled to help substantially if they could be shown a lively interest in the area where the project was located.

The response was encouraging, so much so that a loan was obtained to purchase the Village and start some needed maintenance. Over the years Friends of Hancock Shaker Village have contributed hundreds of thousands of dollars to meet operating expenses. This is quite apart from what many Friends have contributed for the cost of restoration and acquisitions by gift or purchase for the collections.

There have been few tangible advantages in being a Friend. The greatest pleasure, it was felt, was seeing the Village "prosper" as Eldress Emma has vowed. Friends were kept well informed as to the progress and activities at Hancock by way of the semiannual newsletters, being on a preferred mailing list for all special events and in particular, being the guests of honor at the Annual Friends' Day in June.

A Friend recently wrote that he had no idea he would get such a complete education in so many fields since he sent in his original contribution in 1960. He was referring to many distinguished men and women in a wide spectrum of fields who have spoken at Hancock at Friends' Day in June or at a number of conferences and seminars.

The list going back to 1961 is too large to include here. It covers outstanding exponents in restoration and related fields; American history with emphasis on the history of the Shakers, their religion, their music, art, crafts and agriculture.

It has been said by others that in a sense the Friends of Hancock Shaker Village have become the "children" of the childless Shakers, assuring that the spirit of Shakerism will live on even when the few remaining members of the last two communities at Canterbury, New Hampshire, and Sabbathday Lake, Maine, have passed on.

In June of 1981, the trustees, having long felt the need for such an adjunct, established the Council of Friends of Hancock Shaker Village in keeping with provisions in the bylaws.

At a meeting held a few weeks later, Dorothy Walchenbach of Pittsfield was elected chairman of the Council and George Low of Pittsfield was elected secretary. There was no treasurer elected as the expenses of the Council will be carried in the budget of the Village.

The formation of the Council was the recommendation of the committee of the trustees appointed, with John Calkins of Boston, chairman, to recommend special ways to observe the Village's 20th year as a museum. The trustees look forward to the support of the Council of Friends. The topic discussed at its first meeting was plans on how to celebrate the 25th anniversary of the Village.

At Mount Lebanon Emma J. Neale wrote in the *Manifesto*, February, 1878: "In all the great duties of life, let us be mindful that, sands for the mountain and little acts make up the sum of life."

EVENTS AND VISITATIONS

Amateur historians are likely to think of the Shakers as odd, dour, and sometimes unfriendly. Their remoteness in the early years when they were developing their communities intensified this feeling, for they were busily intent on founding their villages and adding to their numbers. While Charles Dickens may not be considered an amateur historian, he described the sect as "grim" on the basis of a brief visit at the New Lebanon (New York) Society, in 1842. He mitigated his criticism somewhat by finding them "good farmers" and "kind and merciful to the brute creature." (He visited them at the end of a long and exhausting lecture tour.)

The business of establishing themselves in a foreign and hostile country, at war with their homeland, and subject to ridicule and brutality, made the Shakers reclusive initially. But there was an element of joy in their worship and they were particularly concerned that as they educated the children in their care, simple diversions and pastimes be included as often as possible with their daily occupations.

Food was important to the Shakers as so much of the work for both sexes was physical. Sisters were taught to regard their endless labors as a fitting opportunity to serve God. This commitment and their feeling of equal responsibility with the men in the family in promoting the health and well-being of the large households resulted in their conviction that a balanced diet was important and that the materials be of outstanding quality. In defining Shaker food and what has made it different, it could be said that it was cooked with refinement and professional skill, though without sectarian predilections; that is, there is no peculiarly "Shaker" cuisine.

The Shakers applied scientific methods in their cooking, and because they worked with large amounts of food they had to estimate and establish weights and measures and relative amounts with care. They were far ahead of their time in their knowledge of nutrition and food values and in creating a special dietary regimen for the elderly and sick.

The brethren, under the direction of the farm deacons, supplied the best possible produce from the immaculate, well-designed gardens and orchards. Vegetables and fruits were grown in great variety and in quantities sufficient to feed more than a hundred people daily. From the large dairies, always shining clean, came buckets of rich milk and cream as well as crocks of golden butter and cheeses superior to any in the neighboring countryside. Bees supplied honey; nuts were harvested from walnut, butternut, and hickory trees on the hillsides, and sugar maple provided syrup, as well as sugar for sale. Each Shaker village was entirely self-sufficient as to fruits, vegetables, chickens and eggs, and all had herds of fine cattle, hogs and sheep and various kinds of domestic grains, supplying all that the family needed for wholesome and varied meals.

It is not surprising that one of the early enterprises approved by the trustees of Shaker Community, Inc., was the forming of the Shaker Kitchen Sisters under the direction of Persis Wellington Fuller, as has already been told. Volunteers headed by Avis Drake Boice operate the "Good Room" adjacent to the Great Kitchen in the Brick Dwelling. Here they sell, on consignment from the best cooks in the area, homemade jams, jellies, pickles, cakes, pies, cookies and a roster of different breads, all in the Shaker tradition. The Good Room is a delicious and tantalizing pause in a tour of the Village and has produced needed and appreciated revenue for the Village. The cooks who supply their delicacies are paid for what they produce, but they also help staff the endeavor on a voluntary basis.

Soon after organizing this group, Mrs. Fuller and others from the Sisters' Good Room began planning for the first Shaker Kitchen Festival,

Events and Visitations / 111

Cooking for visitors: Persis Wellington Fuller in her little white sneakers.

At right, Persis Fuller and Amy Bess Miller, in the kitchen.

August 10-15, 1964. The Great Kitchen had been restored in 1961; now it was expedient to remodel other rooms near it to facilitate the serving of Shaker foods.

Rooms adjoining the old kitchen were spacious when built in 1830 and one of these with wide stone arches, original sand-washed brick walls, flagstone floors, high windows and commodious cupboards was ideal to become the new "Cook Room."

The General Electric Co. in Pittsfield responded generously to an appeal for equipment for the new kitchen. The latest appliances were designed and shipped from GE's Appliance Park in Louisville, Kentucky, to Hancock.

To maintain authenticity the wall ovens were set in brick as were the original bake ovens where Shaker Kitchen Sisters prepared herb breads and "Shaker Loaves" for the community. The new ovens were the latest in modern design and convenience, with automatic controls and precise heating elements that have made it possible for the Village to cook for large numbers of people with ease.

The clean, uncluttered lines of Shaker design were also reflected in the two countertop electric ranges — one set on an island with an overhead hood, the other against a wall. Ranges, the dishwasher and the refrigerator and freezer feature stained wood for a traditional look and the laminated-plastic countertops simulate the scrubbed-wood appearance of birch chopping blocks used in the 19th century.

GE called this operation "an exercise in restraint." But as architects and their clients and editors of periodicals and their photographers continue to stream through the kitchen, it must make the giant corporation proud to have merged the new with the old so successfully.

With such appealing facilities, General Foods Corporation, itself in the vanguard of the American food industry, sponsored the first Shaker Kitchen Festival in 1964; and finding that a beneficial exposure, repeated its backing for the 11th Festival in 1974.

Summer's bounty and the skill of Village cooks, the Good Room Sisters and the Village staff have succeeded in serving Shaker food to thousands of visitors at the World's People Dinners and at daily "tastings" and cooking demonstrations and lectures. Joining General Foods as sponsors of these Festivals have been the following companies:

Borden, Inc., a sponsor in 1969, is a company whose early history was closely tied to the Shakers. Gail Borden, in 1853, developed the process for making sweetened condensed milk. After two years of experimentation Borden, on a visit to the Shaker Community in Mount Lebanon, New York, borrowed a vacuum pan which the Shakers used to concentrate liquid medicines. It was with this pan that he found the first method to condense milk.

The Ball Corporation in 1970 devoted a week to the demonstration of new techniques for preparing and preserving foods, in the Round Stone Barn. The company took this opportunity to show a film daily on the various methods of "setting by" food, as the Shakers would have defined canning, in the 19th century.

The Kraft Corporation during its sponsorship in 1971 developed an attractive six-page folder of recipes inspired by the Shakers' cooking idea. The company also used this week to entertain food editors from across the country at a buffet luncheon. General Foods had done this in 1964. Both companies used the occasion to serve new products soon to be offered to the consumer.

Campbell Soup Company in 1972 also produced a recipe booklet, now a collector's item, and used the Village as background for a film designed for middle- and high-school grades. Every day during the week, in addition to the tastings of Shaker foods, Campbell's soups, chowders and gumbos, hot and cold, were served to visitors.

The Shaker Kitchen Sisters sponsored the 10th Festival in 1973 and brought James Beard, the distinguished author and teacher of culinary arts, to the Village. Mr. Beard, assisted by the late Janet Wertzburger, demonstrated the art of preparing and cooking gourmet food to hundreds of men, women and teen-agers in the Round Stone Barn.

The Corning Company sent the necessary mirror equipment so that everyone in the barn would see. During other parts of the week a bill-of-fare of dishes taken from *The Best of Shaker Cooking* by Village volunteers Persis Fuller and Amy Bess Miller, was tasted. Another feature

Events and Visitations / 113

General Foods Corporation sponsored the first Shaker Kitchen Festival in 1964.

Chocolate-dipping left, was a popular feature of this festival.

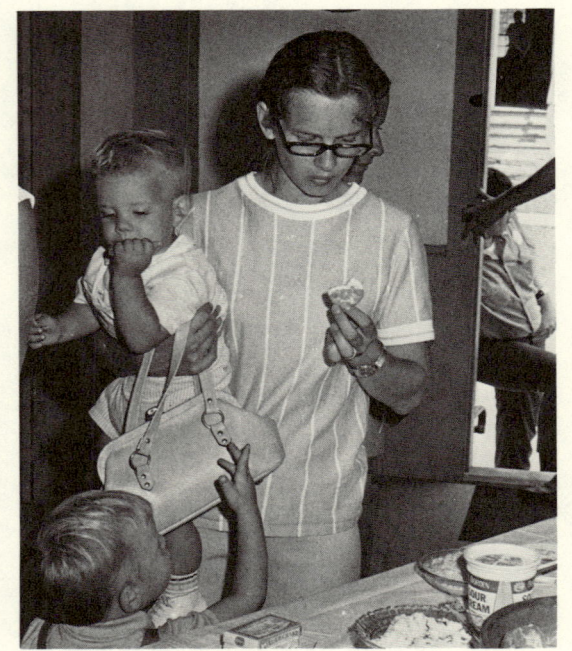

Elsie the Borden cow visited the Round Stone Barn in 1969.

Other samplings at the Borden festival.

Events and Visitations / 115

In 1970, the Ball Corporation gave instruction in preserving food.

Dairy products, sold on the lawn.

during this Festival was the series of morning and afternoon lectures by cookbook writers Jeanne Lessom, Fuller and Miller, all authors published by the Macmillan Company. During this particular Festival week, 760 people were served the World's People's Dinner, including the overseers and trustees of the Boston Symphony Orchestra and the Friends of Tanglewood.

"Visiting historic sites seems to make Americans hungry," wrote Walter Whitehill in his foreword to *The Best of Shaker Cooking* and so it seemed in 1976, the year when the Festival was sponsored by the Adams Super Markets Corporation of Berkshire County. This Festival week featured herbs and how to cook with them, as demonstrated by the Kitchen Sisters in the tastings, as well as how to grow them. There were lectures every day by the Village herbalist in residence, Martha Dahlen, who also demonstrated the technique of drying herbs. Adams Super Markets were pleased as this Festival, which also featured their nutritionist, Penny Knoepel, exceeded the attendance of other years in spite of the threat of gasoline shortages.

In other Festivals there have been demonstrations of bread baking, one year by Jane Nordstrom, the author of two books on the baking of bread, a tour de force when she demonstrated and baked 21 different breads during the week in the Round Stone Barn. Bert Porter of the King Arthur Flour Co., Andover, Massachusetts, a firm founded in 1790, the same year the Shakers organized the community at Hancock, in 1980 baked and commented on "man's great staple" to record audiences in the Barn.

A particularly gala Festival in 1980 featured 12 chefs from Berkshire County restaurants. This area is fortunate in having an outstanding choice of fine country eating places as demonstrated by these professionals. Their specialties covered French, German, English, Greek, Italian, Mexican-American, Chinese and American seafood. All the dishes were cooked and tasted in the Round Stone Barn, accompanied by appropriate beverages.

On June 30, 1888, after a visit to Mount Lebanon, a certain Mrs. Sinclair wrote:

> I never understood before to what perfection the art of cooking can be brought ... it was "plain" cooking made delicious to the palate, tempting to the eye, and as we found, in the highest degree digestible and nutritious. I ought in particular to mention Shaker bread. It is a thing by itself. In the first place, it is light, without being fluffy or spongy... I hope the Shakers will send out missionaries all over the land to teach us to make bread as they make it. Their bread, whether white or brown, is substantial; there is something to it; it is the bread of our mothers (the best of them), only it has a flavor and an eatableness those dear departed ladies seldom attained to. Yet the Shakers eat to live; they do not live to eat. They are temperate in all things, and abstain from everything they believe to be harmful to body or soul.

Mrs. Sinclair recognized 94 years ago the quality of Shaker life as exemplified in one area. It is this quality which the staff and trustees of the Village strive to maintain in all its events. These have a wide range, from the annual Shaker craft festivals to the summer weekly dramatic performances of "An Evening with The Shakers." In this, five members of the Village staff in Shaker garments lead visitors through the Village, talking about long ago occurrences. The evening ends by candlelight in the Believers' Dining Room where Shaker foods are served.

The Holiday Sale held in November is a special event where every part of the Brick Dwelling is arrayed with Shaker-type handmade goods from quilts, knitted goods, other clothing, baskets, boxes, dolls, Shaker furniture from the Industries to every conceivable good thing to eat. A lunch is served and there is a special raffle for the full-size quilt made by the staff during the summer. The net of this one-day sale is over $10,000 to benefit the Village. This is another volunteer-sponsored event.

A visitation and event took place September 3, 1966, when 200 members of the Melville Society visited Hancock in recognition of an afternoon which Melville and Hawthorne spent there in 1851. For this organization's meeting, the Village presented a musical reading of a new American opera, Leonard Kastle's "The Pariahs," which was given its premiere in the Meeting House.

The opera had particular significance for Melville scholars as it was based on the stories of the survivors from the whaling ship *Essex* which was stove in by a whale in the South Pacific in 1822, a theme used in *Moby Dick*. (Later it was repeated for the general public in a program which the Village co-sponsored with the Berkshire Lyric Theatre.) On this September day, the Melville Society had a full tour of the Village and its members were honored at a champagne reception hosted by the Village and its good friend, Dr. Henry A. Murray of Cambridge, noted Melville authority.

Following the restoration of the Great Kitchen and installation of the GE Kitchen, it was possible in 1964 to produce the first of the traditional World's People's Dinners. Invariably sold out, they are presented annually the first week in August during the Kitchen Festival. This concentration on food had its genesis in the Shakers' concern with good nutrition and the preparation of wholesome meals for their large families. Even before 1800 when they experienced some lean times, they often presented gifts of meat and produce to the victims of epidemics and disasters, and throughout the 19th century their prosperous communities fed wayfarers and invited visitors.

As the skill of the earlier Kitchen Sisters became known, city excursionists arrived to share the Shakers' Saturday and Sunday dinners. To the cloistered "Believers," these diners from outside were "the world," and by the mid-19th century "the World's People" were enjoying the Shakers' hospitality in considerable numbers. A brother of the Shaker community at Shirley, Massachusetts, noted this frequent occurrence in his diary in 1883: "A load of the World from Boston today for dinner."

Old accounts mention "great platters of delicious chicken, with yellow gravy," and "Shaker beans, applesauce and cake." But the wise Kitchen Sisters did not plan their meals merely to satisfy bodily hunger and nutrition; their dinners were intended to "create enjoyment, joy and satisfaction to those partaking of them" as well. And sometimes, visitors noted, they would be presented with a farewell gift, one to heighten present joy while promising future satisfaction: a loaf of the Sisters' unforgettable bread.

Not all meals featured chicken, or indeed meat of any kind, for the Shakers followed a vegetarian diet for a period of about 10 years but the "bloodless diet" did not discourage one group of visitors to Hancock's Shaker Brethren over the mountain at Mount Lebanon. Writing "Two Thousand Miles in an Automobile," in 1902, the author known only as "Chauffeur" describes her encounter with the Shakers, and her momentary disappointment in learning that the North Family, with a few exceptions, were strict vegetarians:

> But that dinner was a revelation of what a good cook can do with vegetables in season; It was the quintessence of delicacy, the refinement of finesse, the veritable apotheosis of the kitchen garden; meat would have been brutal, the intrusion of a chop inexcusable, the assertion of a steak barbarous, even a terrapin would have felt quite out of place amidst things so fragrant and palatable as the marvelous preparations of vegetables from that wonderful Shaker Kitchen.
>
> Everything was good, but the various concoctions of sweet corn were better; and such sweet corn! Then the variety of preserves, jellies, and syrups ...
>
> In the cellar we drank something from a bottle labelled "pure grape juice," one of those non-alcoholic beverages with which the teetotaler whips the devil around the stump; another glass would have made Shakers of us all.

The World's People's Dinners, now a revived tradition at Hancock Shaker Village, are intended to perpetuate the culinary integrity and excellence of the sect. Accordingly, the Kitchen Sisters' recipes are being followed as consistently as possible, and the ingredients of each dish are the finest that can be procured. The visitor, of course, is offered no choice of menu in a dinner of this kind, for it is in the style of a hospitable and generous New England farm family whose pleasure is in sharing the bounty of the land.

Writing about the Shakers in 1892, Charles Edson Robinson observed:

> Those who have visited the Shakers in the past, and have been entertained by them in the public dining hall, will recall one feature of the table which was in vogue 35 years ago as a peculiarity of at least the Canterbury Shakers, if of no other Shaker community. On being

ADVICE TO CHILDREN
ON
BEHAVIOUR AT TABLE

First, in the morning, when you rise,
Give thanks to God, who well supplies
Our various wants, and gives us food,
Wholesome, nutritious, sweet, and good:
Then to some proper place repair,
And wash your hands and face with care;
And ne'er the table once disgrace
With dirty hands or dirty face.
When to your meals you have the call,
Promptly attend, both great and small;
Then kneel and pray, with closed eyes,
That God will bless these rich supplies.
When at the table you sit down,
Sit straight and trim, nor laugh nor frown;
Then let the elder first begin,
And all unite, and follow him.
Of bread, then take a decent piece,
Nor splash about the fat and grease;
But cut your meat both neat and square,
And take of both an equal share.
Also, of bones you'll take your due,
For bones and meat together grew.
If, from some incapacity,
With fat your stomach don't agree,
Or if you cannot pick a bone,
You'll please to let them both alone.
Potatoes, cabbage, turnip, beet,
And every kind of thing you eat,
Must neatly on your plate be laid,
Before you eat with pliant blade:
Nor ever—'tis an awkward matter,
To eat or sip out of the platter.
If bread and butter be your fare,
Or biscuit, and you find there are
Pieces enough, then take your slice,
And spread it over, thin and nice,
On one side, only; then you may
Eat in a decent, comely way.
Yet butter you must never spread
On nut-cake, pie, or dier-bread;
Or bread with milk, or bread with meat,
Butter with these you may not eat.
These things are all the best of food,
And need not butter to be good.
When bread or pie you cut or break,
Touch only what you mean to take;
And have no prints of fingers seen
On that that's left—nay, if they're clean.

Be careful, when you take a sip
Of liquid, don't extend your lip
So far that one may fairly think
That cup and all you mean to drink.
Then clean your knife—don't lick it, pray;
It is a nasty, shameful way—
But wipe it on a piece of bread,
Which snugly by your plate is laid.
Thus clean your knife, before you pass
It into plum or apple-sauce,
Or butter, which you must cut nice,
Both square and true as polish'd dice.
Cut not a pickle with a blade
Whose side with grease is overlaid;
And always take your equal share
Of coarse as well as luscious fare.
Don't pick your teeth, or ears, or nose,
Nor scratch your head, nor tonk your toes;
Nor belch nor sniff, nor jest nor pun,
Nor have the least of play or fun.
If you're oblig'd to cough or sneeze,
Your handkerchief you'll quickly seize,
And timely shun the foul disgrace
Of splattering either food or face.
Drink neither water, cider, beer,
With greasy lip or mucus tear;
Nor fill your mouth with food, and then
Drink, lest you blow it out again.
And when you've finish'd your repast,
Clean plate, knife, fork—then, at the last,
Upon your plate lay knife and fork,
And pile your bones of beef and pork:
But if no plate, you may as well
Lay knife and fork both parallel.
Pick up your crumbs, and, where you eat,
Keep all things decent, clean, and neat;
Then rise, and kneel in thankfulness
To Him who does your portion bless;
Then straightly from the table walk,
Nor stop to handle things, nor talk.
If we mean never to offend,
To every gift we must attend,
Respecting meetings, work, or food,
And doing all things as we should.
Thus joy and comfort we shall find,
Love, quietness, and peace of mind;
Pure heavenly Union will increase,
And every evil work will cease.

Events and Visitations / 119

In 1980, Durgin-Park of Boston sponsored a baked bean supper, above.

At right, instruction in making jellies and jams.

seated at the table, a printed sheet was handed to the guest, which might at first be mistaken for a bill of fare, but upon inspection proved to be an injunction.

The "Table Monitor" was written by a Shaker sister, Hannah Bronson, a native of Vermont, who entered the Canterbury community about 1800. It is full of homely yet pertinent truth, and is worthy of reproduction here.

Table Monitor

Gather up the fragments that remain, that nothing be lost.—Christ.

Here, then, is the pattern which Jesus has set,
And his good example we cannot forget;
With thanks for his blessings, his word we'll obey,
But on this occasion we've somewhat to say.
We wish to speak plainly and use no deceit;
We like to see fragments left wholesome and neat;
To customs and fashions we make no pretence,
Yet think we can tell what belongs to good sense.
What we deem good order we're willing to state,
Eat hearty and decent, and clear out our plate;
Be thankful to heaven for what we receive,
And not make a mixture or compound to leave.
We find of those bounties which heaven does give,
That some live to eat, and that some eat to live;
That some think of nothing but pleasing the taste,
And care very little how much they do waste.
Though heaven has blessed us with plenty of food;
Bread, butter, and honey and all that is good;
We loathe to see mixtures where gentle folks dine,
Which scarcely look fit for the poultry or swine.
We often find left on the same China dish,
Meat, apple sauce, pickle, brown bread and minced fish;
Another's replenished with butter and cheese,
With pie, cake and toast, perhaps, added to these.
Now if any virtue in this can be shown,
By peasant, by lawyer, or king on the throne;
We freely will forfeit whatever we've said,
And call it a virtue to waste meat and bread.
Let none be offended at what we here say,
We candidly ask you, is that the best way?
If not, lay such customs and fashions aside,
And if this monitor take, henceforth, for your guide.

Many of the present generation have doubtless heard the expression, "Shaker your plate," and will now appreciate the point of view that brought it into being.

In the fall, Shaker Breakfasts, introduced in 1968 at Hancock, are served in the Believers' Dining Room the last Sunday in September and the first two Sundays in October. These are hearty fare, beginning with cider followed by such rib-stickers as sausage and corn fritters, Shaker breads, jams and jellies, and ending with apple pie and cheese.

Another event concerned with foods compatible with good Shaker cooking was a Baked Bean Supper held for the first time in March 1980, and sponsored by Durgin-Park, the venerable Boston restaurant near Faneuil Hall. One of the three brothers who presently own Durgin-Park, Martin Kelly, arrived at the Brick Dwelling with an assistant chef the afternoon of the supper. Mr. Kelly, who is an enthusiastic skier as well as a bountiful provider, was not fazed by two feet of new snow; his only concern was that with 24 quart-sized beanpots in the back of his car there was no space for his skis.

Each pot was inscribed "Durgin-Park, Boston Baked Beans," and after the supper Mr. Kelly suggested that they could be sold to add to the night's receipts.

Preceding the supper, there was a Baked Bean Bake-Off, a competition of area cooks who entered their special baked beans, judged by those at-

Chef Martin Kelly of Dugin-Park passes judgement on local entries in the Baked Bean Bake-Off Contest, 1980.

tending the suppers. In a field of 28, there were no two pots and contents alike.

It occurred to some that with such hearty appetizers some appetites might fade before the main event, but such was not to be; it proved only to sensitize taste buds. When the last of the two sittings ended with only a few codfish cakes left, only one dish of pickles, a few scraps of home-baked ham and some slices of Boston Brown Bread, also baked in Durgin-Park's ovens, remained. The affair was considered an unqualified success. Apple pies donated by the Village's Kitchen Sisters and staff and mugs of hot coffee sent 180 happy people home, busily discussing baked beans.

The summer of 1962, Mrs. Olive Austin, who as Sister Olive Hayden lived at Hancock for about 20 years, paid an unannounced but special visit to the Village. Mrs. Austin wanted to see her former room, No. 12 on the second floor of the Brick Dwelling. As she went about reminiscing, she attracted an admiring group of visitors who followed her about. She inspected the Village with Dr. Andrews, commenting on the various buildings, their uses and the people who worked in them.

In his book *The Fruits of the Shaker Tree of Life*, Andrews wrote: "The years of absence seemed not to have dimmed her memory, even of details. Her spirit soared. At heart she was a Shakeress again." The staff was moved when just before her departure, in the gathering room of the Dwelling, Mrs. Austin did a little "quick step," singing a Shaker song, as she danced.

The Village is pleased to have one of Mrs. Austin's cherished possessions, a watercolor of the Church Family done by an unknown artist around 1830. It is, as far as is known, the earliest pictorial record of the Village showing the area looking west from the present Trustees' Office to the family dwelling. Some of the buildings are no longer standing, but the painting helped to locate one of the Village wellhouses, which has now been replaced in the proper location. Pictured to the east of the present Brethren's Shop is the boys' shop moved about, now a residence on Route 41.

Not all of the Village's events are food-oriented, although because the Shakers were farmers in a rich and productive area and cooking on a large scale was necessary, this part of their experience necessarily was important. The museum takes advantage of this to give pleasure to its visitors.

The Shakers were skilled mechanics and honest tradesmen. Their reputation in the business community was above reproach and they worked hard to improve "their state." It comes as a surprise to many that they were so well informed, so up to date and so progressive, all because they wanted "to prosper," to use their own phrase. Many letters to the Village trustees ended, "God bless your continued efforts and prosper them." And, "We are asking God to bless your efforts and help you to a happy fulfillment of your carefully laid plans."

The Shakers prospered because of intelligent and well-laid plans and a determination to carry them out. Their elders and eldresses, their deacons and deaconesses, their non-covenanted caretakers and their well-trained sisters and brothers had large responsibilities. All worked hard "to improve their lot," which was the key to survival.

The restored Village has become the locus of many meetings, conferences and gatherings, large and small, because there is far more than passive curiosity and interest in the Shakers and their ways.

An example in the summer of 1966 was a tour of the NEDA Institute in History of the University of Massachusetts. This group, consisting of 127 history teachers from throughout the United States, visited Hancock and 25 other historic sites. The academics were requested to assess the sites on a University-prepared questionnaire. On a scale of 4, the Village scored 3.5, a rating exceeded by only one other site, a restoration project which had been open to the public for many years.

The Institute's report touched on Hancock's overriding attraction: its uniqueness as a place where one may conveniently examine all aspects of a complete society in microcosm. This has long been grasped by students who take advantage of the Village's educational resources. Working with the Village's directors and professional staff over the years have been students from Williams College, Simmons College, Smith College, Mt. Holyoke College, University of Massachusetts, Cornell University and Rensselaer Polytechnic Institute, to name a few. Winter intern programs have allowed both undergraduate and graduate students to pursue projects of mutual research interest and scholarship, often for credit.

The enthusiasm of a group of 44 traveling Danish architects and furniture designers was especially memorable. They delighted in the efficiency of the Village's layout and the uncluttered design of its buildings and artifacts, which they spent a full afternoon sketching and photographing. At Hancock, they said, they discerned more clearly than anywhere else in their travels what most accorded with their sense of the quintessentially *American* qualities of native design.

Because the Village is visited by so many from foreign lands, the 1982 pamphlet guide to the buildings and grounds was translated into French, German, Spanish and Japanese.

Credit and appreciation is extended to Donald Herold, Helga Valigorsky, E. Mario Babarczy and Otohiko Okugawa for this extension of visitor service.

The first sizable conference was held in September 1968, following by a few days the opening of the newly restored Round Stone Barn. Some 150 participants and registrants from throughout the country attended a seminar: "Shakers: A Conference on the Cultural Heritage of an American Communal Sect." Twenty major authorities on Shaker history, thought and works spoke at six sessions, a three-day event concluded with a tour of the former Shaker settlements at Tyringham, Massachusetts, Mount Lebanon, and Canaan, New York, as well as the Shaker Museum at Old Chatham, New York.

Among those present were representatives from the Philadelphia Museum of Art, the New York State Museum, the Museum of American Folk Art, the Detroit Institute of Arts, Old Sturbridge Village, and the Henry Francis DuPont Winterthur Museum. Four of the sessions were held at Hancock in the newly restored carriage wing of the barn; the others were conducted at the Darrow School, a preparatory school occupying the former Shaker community at Mount Lebanon, New York, where the conference registrants were housed.

The conference was in part supported by the Carl A. Weyerhaeuser Family Trust, which was established in 1961 and is now used to memorialize the interests of the late Mrs. Maud Moon Weyerhaeuser Sanborn, friend of the Village whose generosity has been cited previously.

An event of major importance took place on July 18, 1969, when the Village in its ninth year was designated a National Historic Landmark by the National Park Service of the U.S. Department of the Interior. Informing the Village of the certification, the Secretary of the Interior, Stewart Udall wrote, "Your project at Hancock has been found to possess exceptional value in commemorating and illustrating the history of the United States."

Some events were of international importance and were responsible for greater influx than usual of foreign visitors. In 1969 the Village staff under Eugene Dodd, curator, worked all summer to prepare an exhibition which was shipped to Japan for the United States Pavilion at Expo '70, the international exposition which would open in March 1970, on the Senri Hills near Osaka. The exhibition, commissioned by the U.S. Information Agency, was one of the major attractions of the Pavilion and occupied a central area of 500 square feet. In addition, the Round Barn was featured in a photographic exhibition at Expo documenting the functionalism permeating the American architectural tradition.

This was not the first international exposition to feature Shaker artifacts in an American pavilion. In 1958 a small but representative collection of Shaker boxes was loaned to the United States exhibition at Brussels, Belgium, to be included in a display of early Americana. The collector has since given this collection to Hancock Shaker Village.

During the winter of 1964, plans were completed for the first public event outside the Village to benefit the restoration, specifically the Round Stone Barn. A preview to be held April 16 had been arranged by Mr. and Mrs. Edward Fowles, friends of the Village and owners of Duveen Brothers Art Gallery on 79th Street, New York City, where the event took place. The occasion was the display of a remarkable collection of rare English silver belonging to Lord Richard Brownlow, lifelong friend of the late Duke of Windsor.

It was to be dispersed at Christie's in London, but because of its exceptionally high quality, it was decided to put on view in New York, before the sale, many pieces with a royal provenance and described as "the most important of its kind and part of the riches of the centuries." Christie's announced from London, "No collection has ever before been flown to America prior to its being auctioned, and this will be the most valuable consignment of silver ever to cross the Atlantic."

The benefit was a great success as a fundraiser and equally important in making many new friends for the Village and publicizing the dangerous state of the Barn. Lord and Lady Brownlow were guests of honor and showed interest in the fact that the founder of the United Society of Believers, Ann Lee, was an Englishwoman.

Trustees and Friends of the Village were so elated with the success of the benefit that plans were perfected during the winter of 1965 to hold a "Save-the-Barn Day" July 17, 1965, at the Village with the emphasis heavily on all the rural aspects of the Village.

First to offer to help in any way possible were Eric Sloane, well-known illustrator, artist and Americana author and good friend of the Village; and Mr. and Mrs. Samuel G. Colt Jr., who were chairmen of the event. Sloane spent the day autographing his books, with profits going to save the Barn, and in the late afternoon officiated at the drawing of the winning raffle ticket for his oil painting of the Barn. He had long been concerned with the aesthetic beauty of the handsome building now crumbling and no longer able to survive on historical fame and good wishes.

The 4-H Club members had been selling raffle tickets for months and on the big day they exhibited five breeds of cattle: Jersey, Guernsey, Brown Swiss, Holstein and Red Polled to 500 supporters of the Barn. Haymaker's switchel, roasted ears of corn, and crackers and cheese were sold to families bringing their picnic lunches. At noon and again at 1:30 a World's People's Dinner was served in the Believers'

124 / Hancock Shaker Village

Hancock Shaker Village's Exhibit at Expo '70 in Osaka, Japan, top left.

Above, crossing Route 20 from one lecture to another.

Events and Visitations / 125

A Crafts Fair demonstration, top.

The Osaka exhibit.

Dining Room. Both sittings were oversold.

As a result of these two events on behalf of the Barn, more than $16,000 was raised to stem the ravages of the elements.

Plans for the celebration of the Shaker Bicentennial were being made several years before the actual commemorative date of August 6, 1774, when Mother Ann Lee and eight of her followers landed in New York City. It was observed in different ways in different areas where there was serious interest in the Shakers. At Hancock, to mark this significant date, the staff and trustees tried to perfect already established procedures, initiate new and interesting programs which illustrate the Shaker way of life and stress the benefits which come to us from this life style.

The National Broadcasting Company asked Amy Bess Miller to be on its morning "Today" program on August 6, 1974, the birthday of Mother Ann, founder of the Shaker sect. Tom Davenport, who had filmed and produced a documentary film, "The Shakers," was also on the show. It took more than a week to answer all the resultant letters and cards received from those who saw the program and who had visited Hancock or who knew about the Shakers' history.

In the fall of the same year, Dr. Russell Barber, whose NBC program on religion was produced for Sunday viewings at the noon hour, asked the Village to participate. Dr. Barber wanted to talk about the religion of the Shakers, among others, and as it was to be aired the Sunday before Thanksgiving, he wanted to emphasize their success as farmers, and as providers for large families with accent on their cookery, which Dr. Barber thought was almost as much admired as Shaker furniture.

He proposed that the Village should transport to his studio the complete background of a Shaker dining room, tables and chairs and all the holiday food of a 19th-century New England family. It was agreed that the Village would exercise suitable Shaker restraint and that all the dishes would be cooked from authentic Shaker recipes which had been printed in *The Best of Shaker Cooking.*

The Good Room Kitchen Sisters, under Persis Fuller's direction with Janet Viner and Frances Persip Duval doing the cooking, rallied to the

Jerry V. Grant, now the Village's director, demonstrating box-making in Boston.

challenge. John Ott and his staff put together a model room and selected furniture and artifacts from the Village's collections. A rented outsize station wagon was loaded the night before, and early in the morning of the filming Veola Lederer and Amy Bess Miller left for New York and the NBC studio. The studio crew set up the room using 15 feet of pegboard from which hung sisters' cloaks. They unpacked china and glass and arranged a long table, a cupboard and several chairs, but the crew's real curiosity was in the food which they had been told they could sample at the end.

To begin the program, Barber and Miller discussed the coming of the Shakers to America, their origins, religious beliefs and communal living. The camera turned then to the table, and the menu was discussed: a Berkshire turkey from the Burgner Farm in Pittsfield, with sage stuffing and chestnut gravy; Shaker squash and tomatoes with brown sugar and chives; corn fritters and maple syrup; a variety of pickles and relishes in glass compotes; spiced crabapples; jams and jellies and a variety of breads; cider in glass pitchers; an assortment of cookies and small cakes; two-layer cakes on pedestal cake dishes; a mince pie and an Ohio lemon pie; and several old-fashioned cheeses.

A colorful arrangement of fruits in a Shaker basket was in the middle of the table and Good Room breads were on the lip of the cupboard waiting to be cut.

It took over an hour to set the stage. The taping was done in 40 minutes, and the crew finished the food in 15 minutes and went on to the next show, but with high praise for the culinary standards of the Good Room Sisters. The response from this show was a general increase in reservations for all dinners and breakfasts for the World's People.

Another Shaker bicentennial observance was a three-day convention in Cleveland, Ohio, in October, 1974. There were 225 Shaker enthusiasts attending, and the guests of honor were Eldress Gertrude M. Soule, Eldress Bertha Lindsay and Sister Miriam Wall.

The program was varied and immensely interesting. Some of the convention topics were: "Spiritual Lineage of Shakerism," "Shakers in American History, 1774-1850," "Shaker Herbs,"

"New Insight on Shakers," "The Western Shakers," "Shaker Architecture," "Shaker Cooking," and "Shaker Manuscripts and Bibliography."

Among the speakers were: Don Yoder, University of Pennsylvania; Mario DePillis, University of Massachusetts; Amy Bess Miller, Hancock Shaker Village; Daniel W. Patterson, University of North Carolina; Charles van Ravenswaay, Winterthur Museum; Mary C. Black, New York Historical Society; Robert Meader, Shaker Museum, Old Chatham, New York; Bertram Wyatt-Brown, Case Western Reserve University; Daniel Porter, Ohio Historical Society; Mary Lou Conlin, Shaker Historical Society, Cleveland; John C. Poppeliers, Historic American Buildings Survey; William Talbot, Cleveland Museum of Art; Kermit J. Pike, Western Reserve Historical Society; and Mary L. Richmond, librarian, Williamstown, Massachusetts.

The convention concluded with a two-day bus tour of the Union Village area at Lebanon, Ohio, and the Shakertown settlement at Pleasant Hill, Kentucky, with Eldress Gertrude Soule and Eldress Bertha Lindsay and Sister Miriam Wall aboard.

Prior to the Ohio convention, a three-day conference, August 3-6, had taken place at Sabbathday Lake, Maine, at the Shaker community there. It was the result of more than a year's planning by the Shaker sisters and Theodore E. Johnson, director of the Shaker Museum there, and it was highlighted by the presentation of scholarly papers on different aspects of Shaker history and theology. All the sessions took place in the lovely 1794 Meeting House.

The Shakers in the West Pittsfield and Hancock families had their own post office at this eastern end of the community. In August 1854, August W. William, elder of the East Family, was appointed postmaster, and held the position until 1888. It is hoped that as the remaining restoration is completed at Hancock, a postal substation serving not only the Village but the communities of West Pittsfield and Richmond adjacent to it, can be re-established at the Village.

On Friday, August 6, 1976, a long-anticipated ceremony took place in the Round Stone Barn. It commemorated not only Mother Ann's birthday, but it observed the bicentennial of our country. Congressman Silvio O. Conte, long a

Shaker craftsmanship was honored during the bicentennial.

helpful supporter of the Village, had worked for two years to have the Shakers included in the series honoring The American Craftsman. A 13-cent United States Postal Service embossed envelope was first issued at Lanesboro, where Hancock mail is distributed, and then first-day covers were sold at the Round Stone Barn. The bell at the Dwelling House rang out as it had on the fourth of July and called 200 guests to the ceremony. Joseph H. Nolan, Pittsfield postmaster, presided and Andrew Clarke, director of the Berkshire Chorale Society, led the company in singing our national anthem.

The Reverend Bryce T. Cleveland of the Hancock Baptist Church gave the invocation and Donald F. Griffin, postmaster of Lanesboro, welcomed the guests, and Mrs. Lawrence K. Miller, president of Shaker Community, Inc., introduced the distinguished visitors. Remarks were made by Eldress Gertrude M. Soule from the Central Ministry of the United Society of Believers, Canterbury, New Hampshire, and Representative Conte. Sister Miriam Wall from Canterbury was in the audience and was also introduced.

Postmaster Nolan introduced William F. Bolger, deputy postmaster general, later postmaster general, who gave the address and presented handsome albums prepared by the U.S. Postal Service and containing the envelope, designed by Arthur Congdon, featuring a Shaker rocker. The benediction was given by the Reverend Thomas N. Westhoven, S.C.J., director, Dehon Seminary, Lanesboro.

Following the ceremonies, the trustees of the Village honored the platform guests at luncheon in the Believers' Dining Room of the Brick Dwelling. As a keepsake to mark the occasion, the guests were each given copies of the Village's first history-guidebook, written by director John H. Ott. Its pictures and maps and detailed survey of each building are a great addition to the interpretation and better understanding of life within the Church Family during its 170 years' existence.

The event was described fully in *Stamp: The Weekly Magazine of Philately* in a timely article by Leo Lincoln, Berkshire County's indefatigable stamp authority. He remarked in his opening paragraph: "Possibly for the first time on record, a first-day-of-issue exercises for a U.S. Government stamp were held in a barn."

From 1961 to the present, there have been people, in groups and individually, who have come to Hancock Shaker Village for a myriad of reasons and purposes. Almost all in some way or another have been instructive or of benefit to the Village.

One of the first visitations was from The Club of Odd Volumes of Boston on October 7, 1961. The members were on their way to Marlboro (Vermont) College for a special convocation the next day, when an honory master of arts degree would be given one of their members, Rudolph Ruzicka, internationally known graphic artist and designer.

The guests were first conducted on a tour of the Village which ended in the Brick Dwelling where Dr. Andrews had arranged a special exhibition of books and pamphlets published by Shaker communities. Shown in the Gathering Room were 18 Shaker-imprint items. Earliest of the publications was one from Lebanon, Ohio, dated 1808 and classified as extremely rare. It was *The Testimony of Christ's Second Appearing*, the standard work on Shaker theology. These publications are now in the Village library.

Dr. Andrews had also prepared a keepsake for the honored guests. It was a poem by Isaac N. Youngs of the New Lebanon (New York) Society. He was one of those versatile craftsmen so commonly found among the Shakers. On entering the dairy and observing the making of cheese he wrote:

> *Look if you please*
> *On yonder cheese*
> *Flowers so fine I see*
> *Leaves of sage*
> *Set by a gauge*
> *For superfluity*
> *I'm sure such cheese makers*
> *Cannot be Shakers*

Many important Village-related events take place elsewhere. Among them are exhibitions of Shaker furniture and artifacts which have traveled far from home. In 1973, the Village's entire collection of Spirit Drawings, and seven pieces of furniture were included in a special Shaker exhibit at the Renwick Gallery of the Smithsonian Institution in Washington, opening November 1.

The Club of Odd Volumes of Boston, at the Round Stone Barn in 1961.

In February 1974, a number of pieces from the Village's collections were included in an exhibition of Shaker material, furniture and artifacts from American museums to tour in Europe, sponsored by the Department of State. Museums included were in Munich, Zurich, Vienna, Copenhagen, Stockholm, Goteborg and London, where the exhibition was scheduled to end in May 1975. However, the traveling collection was so successful that the tour was extended to museums in Vienna, West Berlin, Paris, Lisbon and Warsaw.

Several trustees saw at firsthand the enthusiastic reception of these Shaker pieces. Viewing the collection at the Victoria and Albert Museum in London were John Ott, Carl Weyerhaeuser and Amy Bess Miller. Ott and Miller also went to Paris with Carl and Charles Weyerhaeuser the next year, where the collection was housed at the Musee des Arts Decoratifs in the Louvre. In 1977, just before it returned to its country of origin, Lawrence and Amy Bess Miller went to Lisbon, where they were joined by Carl Weyerhaeuser and his son, Charles. They were entertained by the U.S. ambassador at the Gulbenkian Museum, where the exhibition was shown.

A step forward for the Village was the addition to the staff of June Sprigg, as curator of collections. No sooner had she arrived in the early summer of 1977 than she plunged into preparing exhibitions for the Statehouse in Boston and at the University of Connecticut's William Benton Museum of Art at Storrs.

The latter exhibition opened with a reception March 20 and featured more than 150 of the Village's finest examples of baskets, furniture, tools and textiles. It focused on the excellence of Shaker design and workmanship while exploring the Shakers' place among America's utopian communities of the past two centuries. A series of films, special events and lectures accompanied the show, spread over the following weeks. They included a dance presentation by Cheryl Anderson and a slide talk by June Sprigg entitled, "Shakers and their Visitors: 'Zion' meets the 'World'; What did tourists Charles Dickens, Nathaniel Hawthorne, Ralph Waldo Emerson, and the Marquis de Lafayette say about their trips to Shaker Villages?"

"The Gift of Inspiration: Art of the Shakers, 1830-80" opened at the Hirschl & Adler Galleries, New York, May 3, 1979, and ran through May 25 as a benefit for the Village. Hilton Kramer, art critic of the *New York Times* said, "One of the sweetest and most delicate forms of 19th-century American folk art is the so-called 'spirit drawing' of the Shakers and we are given an unusual opportunity to see some of the classic examples of this genre in the exhibition."

The show was based primarily on Hancock's outstanding collection of spirit drawings, but there were more than 20 institutions and individuals who also loaned from their collections to make it the most comprehensive showing of Shaker art to date. It was the first Shaker show to include maps, landscapes, village views, architectural renderings, and other practical works, and was the first to contrast Shaker art and the worldly folk art of the Shakers' New England neighbors.

A 70-page catalog with some 40 illustrations was designed by William Sosa of *The Berkshire Eagle* and printed in Dalton, Massachusetts, by the Studley Press. It was "dedicated to Eldress Emma B. King and Sister Miriam Wall and to 21 former trustees and generous benefactors, none of whom are living, but who in important ways have made the project a reality." Essays by Nina Fletcher Little, noted authority on American folk art, and June Sprigg, curator of collections at Hancock, were included in the catalog. The Village appreciated the opportunity afforded by Norman Hirschl and Stuart P. Feld for their generosity in offering their galleries for this special event and for underwriting the printing of the catalog. The exhibit attracted 300 to the preview and hundreds thereafter during the next three weeks.

No one was more helpful to the Village as it struggled for recognition than Professor Charles R. Keller, at one time a Village trustee, director of the John Hay Fellows and a former Williams College faculty member. For several years Professor Keller brought hundreds of high school teachers and administrators to the Village under the John Hay Program which concentrated on informal summer immersions in the humanities, housing the conferees for a month at Williams College. There were tours of the Village, lectures and a bountiful World's People's Dinner for these visitors each July, and it was a sad day when after 13 years the program closed in 1966.

One event must be mentioned in particular. Mrs. Ludwig Lederer, long-time trustee and vice president of the Board of Trustees, in 1980 commissioned a Shaker musical work by Janet Green Catlin to celebrate the 20th year of Hancock Shaker Village as a museum, and also to honor Amy Bess Miller, her old friend and co-worker at the Village.

A delightful performance of *The Singing Tree* was held in the 1910 Barn on a mild July evening with Richmond and Lenox mountains as a backdrop through the open barn doors. The auditors, who had been dinner guests of Mrs. Lederer and John and Lili Ott at the Brick Dwelling, sat in what was formerly the spacious hayloft and marveled at the perfect acoustics. The play, an imaginative evocation of a Shaker experience, played before a capacity seated audience of 100, was based on authentic Shaker songs and words, except for one song composed by the author. The evening was a perfect example of the adaptability of Village buildings.

The 1880-1910-1939 complex of three barns is the locus of the Shaker Community Industries, but for this memorable occasion, thanks to Veola Lederer, wise counselor, thoughtful and generous supporter of all aspects of the Village, the hayloft was adapted for dramatic use with remarkable effect.

This small auditorium is a welcome addition to other covered spaces in the Village for exhibitions, lectures or larger seminars.

One of the most enthusiastic and appreciative visitors the Village ever had was Mrs. Lyndon B. Johnson. Lady Bird received an honorary degree at Williams College and in the citation President John E. Sawyer spoke of her "quiet leadership and powerful moral support for deeply humane causes, ranging from project Head Start to the quality of the total environment in which we live."

The next day, October 9, 1967, interrupting a busy schedule en route to Yale University where she was to speak that evening, Mrs. Johnson spent two hours touring the Village, examining nearly all the restored buildings as well as the Round Stone Barn, which at that time was awaiting restoration. She expressed warm approval for all the programs which the Village was undertaking and gave those involved a special impetus to carry on the work.

After Shaker cookies in the Good Room, the Village staff presented her with a reproduction Shaker child's chair, which she said would be reserved for her grandson Patrick's visits to the White House. Since leaving the White House, on two separate unannounced visits Mrs. Johnson returned to inspect later phases of the restoration.

In *A White House Diary*, Mrs. Johnson wrote:

> We arrived at the Shaker Village and Mrs. Lawrence Miller took us through, with a sizable crowd of press and members of her restoration committee. In this unique settlement, members of the Shaker religious cult had lived and worked and worshiped for about 170 years. The last of them, a few elderly women, had sold the land and buildings in 1960 to a restoration group and now they are open to the public. The Shakers lived apart from the world, got up before daylight, worked hard as farmers and as craftsmen of fine plain furniture, and lived a life of celibacy. Members of this sect were early gatherers, packagers, and sellers of seeds, vegetables and flowers. (The latter they used, alas, only for medicinal purposes.) They had sold seeds as far afield as every state in the Union, and to London, and even Australia.

In October 1975, the Village was asked to mount an exhibition demonstrating unique pieces of Shaker furniture at the most important of the New England antique shows, The Ellis Memorial, which benefits the organization of that name.

The arrangements were superbly executed by a Village trustee, John Calkins, who to give the Village even more exposure arranged a reception following a Sunday viewing, at the observatory at the top of I.M. Pei's stunning John Hancock Building in Boston.

John Ott described the Hancock restoration to a keen audience and there was speculation that from the commanding height, the landscape viewed could include the Shaker Villages at Sabbathday Lake, Maine, and Canterbury, New

Hampshire, to the north, the abandoned communities at Harvard and Shirley, Massachusetts, to the immediate west, and just possibly by bounce-back, the restored Hancock Shaker Village in the Berkshires.

In 1974, the month of January was one of the coldest on record and in addition, coal and heating oil were in short supply and expensive. It was not surprising that the huge Seventh Regiment Armory on Park Avenue at 67th Street registered a chilly 48 degrees as antique dealers unpacked their wares for the Winter Antiques Show which since its start in 1954 has annually benefited the East Side Settlement House.

The Village was pleased and proud to be asked to provide the exhibition for the very center of this enormous showplace of antiquities. It was considered a rare opportunity to tell the story of the restoration at Hancock. Village trustee Joseph D. Ryle had encouraged John Ott, director of the Village, to undertake the planning, which began in March of the year before.

It was decided to exhibit a Brethren's Kitchen and Herb Garden which would afford an opportunity to display some unusual Shaker tools, a beehive, an assortment of baskets, a bench and, of course, a variety of plants used by the Shaker Sisters in cooking and in herbal medicines at Hancock. It was also conceived as a welcome anodyne to the fierce winter weather.

The area allotted to the garden was enclosed with a three-rail white fence. There were three openings for crosswalks and the public was invited to enter the garden and look at the plants and read placards describing the use of the herbs in the days of the Shakers and also to pick up literature about the Village.

A design was submitted to Adelma G. Simmons, good friend of the Village, who had helped several years before in the planning of the herb gardens at Hancock. Mrs. Simmons also agreed not only to supply the plants needed, but with John Ott and Amy Bess Miller she spent seven hours planting them. It was the first time these three had planted a garden wearing woolen mittens. Philip Clarke and Walter Pictrowski brought the Shaker material and a load of loam to the Armory in a truck and did a lot of the spade work. All was in good shape for the preview of this elegant show by 5 o'clock.

That summer many who came to look at the herb gardens at the Village had been first made aware of the importance of the Shaker herb industry when they saw the small garden at the Winter Antiques Show.

The herb garden design for the New York Winter Antiques Show, 1974.

MAJOR DONORS

The two questions most often asked the trustees by antiquarians, are: Who paid for the restoration of the Village and how is the operation of the Village annually financed? Generally, a large restoration project has a principal donor.

Was there not some spiritual or conservative religious interest involved? Was there a tax advantage to be gained by some rich well-wisher? Was not some affluent history buff interested? Was not some well-heeled collector of Shaker furniture and artifacts in the wings aspiring to show his collections to best advantage? Was there not a rags-to-riches native son wishing to celebrate nostalgically the virtues of hard physical labor, sobriety and the religious impulses of the 19th-century Village, although overlooking the communitarian aspects of the followers of Mother Ann Lee?

No, there was no single benefactor who gave the incorporators extra courage. They undertook the risk without an angel in the wings when they borrowed the purchase price for the Village from a bank. In retrospect, it might have been the very absence of such an individual that steeled the founders' determination and audacity, impressing the immediate Berkshire community and later impressing the boards of national foundations. Nor was there any state or federal money involved at the outset.

Also in retrospect there were several examples of similar ventures, however financed. In addition, the climate was right in Massachusetts and New England. The Trustees of Reservations in Massachusetts and the Society for the Preservation of New England Antiquities have been a force in historic preservation by private impulse since the late 19th century.

As to private donors in this field, Henry Ford in the 1920s created Greenfield Village in Dearborn, Michigan. A few years later Colonial Williamsburg, a meticulous reconstruction on an historic site in Virginia, was planned and totally financed by John D. Rockefeller Jr. and his family. And while it was not a village, Henry Francis Du Pont opened to the public his gardens and house at Winterthur, filled with treasures, now a vast teaching museum. In Winston-Salem, North Carolina, there is the fascinating Moravian village called Old Salem which has been reclaimed and restored by members of the Reynolds family.

In the Northeast the Wells family of Southbridge in central Massachusetts, wishing to house their splendid collections of early Americana in a proper setting, began moving period houses, stores, and other structures until an entire early 19th-century village was recreated, known as Old Sturbridge Village. In Old Deerfield, Massachusetts, Mr. and Mrs. Henry N. Flynt had acquired the beautiful 18th-century village on the Connecticut River. It had been beleaguered by the Indians and was the site of an historic massacre, but happily its lovely early houses had not been destroyed. The Flynts restored each house over a period of years, furnishing each one suitably and with taste, opening them as they were completed, until this entire charming Connecticut Valley village was open to the public.

In Shelburne, Vermont, a few miles south of Burlington, Mrs. J. Watson Webb assembled a large group of disparate structures to house her collections of Americana. Of all the outdoor museums, this offers the greatest variety, for there one can board the *S.S. Ticonderoga*, which plied the waters of Lake Champlain until it was moved permanently to the shores of the Village, and a few yards away visit an imposing Greek revival mansion in which are incorporated the rooms of Mrs. Webb's New York apartment furnished with its contents. In between are buildings of various periods, a formal museum of works by American artists of the 19th and early 20th century, a Shaker carriage barn from Canterbury, New Hampshire, full of farm tools, and a magnificent structure which houses a collection of elegant horse-drawn carriages, to mention only a portion of the whole.

The answer to the second question — who supports Hancock Village today — is easy. It is those who visit the Village for one reason or another, some 6,000 in the winter months for workshops and classes, and more than 50,000 during six months in the summer. Their admission and class fees cover roughly one-third of the operating budget.

Another third is made up of the revenue from the shops — comestibles from the Good Room in the Brick Dwelling, the Fancy Goods store at the Trustees' Office, and Herb Shop in the barn complex, and the Bookstore in the Visitors' Center. The Lunch Shop, also in the Visitors' Center does not run at a profit, but neither does it lose money. The Community Industries Program, recently launched, is expected to produce revenue once fully under way.

The remaining sources of funds to balance the budget are special events and the Friends of Hancock Shaker Village, now numbering more than a thousand. This group is generous with its contributions and in providing volunteers for special events and regular operations.

Periodically, the Village has received special grants from federal and state governments to support the operation and special programs. These cannot be relied upon for continued support, however.

In our country, going back to 1892 when the Trustees of Reservations was formed in Massachusetts, there has been an increasing interest in the strands from which the fabric of our national culture has been woven. One of the "conspicuous strains" in our history, as Constance Rourke has pointed out in *Roots of American Culture*, has been the "impulse toward communal organization" in the settlements of the Pilgrims and the frontier hamlets, in the Mennonite and Amish communities, in the idealistic experiments at Brook Farm, Fruitlands, Amana, New Harmony, Old Economy, Oneida, and the many Fourieristic phalanxes — even the Mormons.

It was evident in 1959 when the Village at Hancock was closed by the Society of Shakers, that there was a grass-roots interest in one of the most productive and more long-lived associations, the United Society of Shakers. It was widely appreciated that these people had done so much to give beauty, strength and distinction to the national character and that it was a work of the highest importance to preserve and memorialize their contributions, both material and spiritual.

The initial appeal for funds was in the form of a letter from the trustees dated September 10, 1960. It was sent to 300 individuals who were either in a position to help financially or to interest others and to spread the word about the intentions of the trustees.

This appeal formally launched a capital campaign to buy, restore and operate as a museum the Shaker Community. The amount sought was $250,000. It was learned later that one sentence in the letter persuaded individuals to respond. It said, "Foundations are more readily impelled to help substantially if they can be shown a lively interest in the area where the project is located, an enthusiasm among the academic community concerned in the field involved, and a disposition among individuals of spirit, affection and understanding to help in this exciting preservation."

The reply in a remarkably short period in cash or short-term pledges from individuals was over $97,000, sufficient to pay the bank interest and support a staff of three and some essential maintenance and repairs, and take the first steps in formulating restoration policy and guidelines to be undertaken by professionals in the field.

The response to the cry for help in the saving of this chapter of American cultural history came from many sides. Volunteers turned up in numbers to help tidy up the grounds. An enthusiastic but still anonymous donor after talking with one of the workmen gave him a hundred-dollar bill. After a longer tour about the property, he gave the same man two more hundred-dollar bills and said, "You sure do need it." This guaranteed the payroll for two weeks.

Late in 1961 at the close of the day Philip Clark was stretched out beside one of the herb beds weeding it with a large screwdriver. Two visitors coming upon him asked if it wouldn't be easier if he had a hoe to weed with. He answered, "Sure, if we had the money to buy one." In a few

Faith and Edward D. Andrews at Hancock viewing materials from their collection.

136 / Hancock Shaker Village

William L. Lassiter at one of the Kitchen Festivals.

days these good Berkshire County neighbors sent the treasurer a check for $4,000.

No part of the cost of early restoration ever came out of operating funds. It was all underwritten by individuals or foundations, some with Berkshire connections, some without.

In 1965 Carleton Sherwood of New York was engaged to publicize the critical state of the Round Stone Barn and a brochure was distributed for the first time outside the Berkshire area to a much larger group interested in the preservation of fine old buidings and the history of the Shakers. A group, headed by Eric Sloane, the well-known artist, known as the Save-the-Barn Committee, was formed and its immediate efforts raised the $16,000 needed to shore up the failing structure and keep it intact pending complete restoration. The eight-page brochure written by Robert B. Kimball of Richmond, printed by the Excelsior Press of North Adams at cost, on paper donated by the Rising Company of Housatonic, both generous Berkshire neighbors, featured the crumbling Barn with the caption "Village Landmark Crumbling." It read:

> Most acute of all the preservation problems at Hancock Shaker Village are those involving the village's landmark, the 1826 Round Stone Barn. Crumbling with the years and the inroads of weather, though shored and propped and heated above freezing as a winter safeguard, the massive structure needs major reconstruction so that it can be opened safely to the public. Individuals from widely scattered parts of the nation are giving money earmarked for the project, but the cost of restoration goes beyond the scope of small, personal gifts. Estimates on thorough rebuilding range into several hundred thousand dollars.

Frederick W. Beinecke let it be known to several of the Village trustees that "as soon as I fulfill my commitment to building the Beinecke Library at Yale I'll see what can be done about the Barn." The rare-books library at Yale was dedicated April 10, 1965, the gift of Edward, Frederick and Walter Beinecke. Fritz Beinecke gave the word to start restoration proceedings for the Barn in the fall of 1967.

Different stimuli motivate the gift of giving. Edith Rosenwald Stern said that she and her husband, Edgar, happened quite by chance to see an exhibition of Shaker furniture, probably at the Berkshire Museum, and she always wanted to know how these "reclusive" people lived and furnished their houses. Maud Sanborn was a discerning collector of Shaker furniture which as a summer resident had led her on numerous buying outings. Both she and her son Carl wanted to see the Village saved.

Winthrop M. Crane Jr. was helpful; he had a prior interest in the Lebanon School for Boys established in the Mount Lebanon Shaker Village.

Mrs. Thomas (Margaret) Blodgett, a neighbor in Great Barrington, was generous, enthusiastic and sympathetic and as the others did, gave often before serious restoration got under way in order to keep the project from failing before it had a chance to succeed. She recognized the need for research, for which she established a fund.

Early supporters were motivated for different reasons. Many of the trustees had been collectors of Shaker furniture and artifacts. They had started in the early 1920s to buy from the Shakers themselves. One of the Village's founding trustees, and generous friend, Dorothy Miller Cahill, tells of visiting at Mount Lebanon and after a prolonged tour of several buildings, the gentle sister asked if there were any other things she could show her. Rather timidly she said yes. Whereupon, she was shown some choice furniture: a cupboard, a fine table and other pieces which she purchased and which she has enjoyed ever since.

William Laurence Lassiter came to the Village first as a volunteer — weekly and sometimes daily during the Kitchen Festivals, Friends' Days or other special events. He had known the Hancock, Mount Lebanon and Watervliet Shaker families, as had his mother. Many of the Watervliet Society recipes in "The Best of Shaker Cooking" by Miller and Fuller were chosen from his mother's collection.

As curator of history and art at the New York State Museum in Albany, Lassiter helped form the museum's Shaker collections. He was also the author of two books on the Shakers that are still in print: "Shaker Architecture" and "Shaker Recipes and Formulas for Cooks and Homemakers."

Maud Moon Weyerhaeuser Sanborn, dear friend and enthusiastic collector of Shaker artifacts and history.

PUBLICATIONS AND PUBLICITY

Eldresses Anna White and Leila S. Taylor of the North Family at Mount Lebanon, New York, write in their *Shakerism: Its Meaning and Message* (1904) that during the first 75 years of their communal existence the Shakers were too busy with temporal conditions and spiritual needs "to engage in literary or artistic enterprises." They said that Shaker literary skill did not reveal itself in the world's markets, but wanting to be honest, they qualified this by saying: "Shakers have left behind much in art and literature commonly regarded as of value." This is an understatement.

J.P. MacLean's Shaker bibliography of books, pamphlets and broadsides published in 1905 includes 523 titles. In 1977 Mary L. Richmond, Village trustee and former librarian of the Chapin Library at Williams College, compiled a bibliography of Shaker material containing 1,727 entries in the first volume of primary matter and 2,381 entries in the second of secondary material. The Village was proud to be able to raise the funds to subsidize this outstanding work, published by the University Press of New England, Durham, New Hampshire.

It was in character with Shaker tradition when in 1959 Mr. and Mrs. Carl P. Rollins prepared a report for the Steering Committee (soon to become the Board of Trustees of Shaker Community, Inc.) urging the trustees to adopt at once a strong policy of publication. They felt this was so important it should proceed simultaneously with the restoration of the buidings and grounds. They presented a list for consideration. The Rollinses guided the design and production of all early publications by Shaker Community, Inc., establishing high typographical standards. Mr. Rollins, a founding trustee, died in 1960. Mrs. Rollins, also a trustee, continued to be actively involved almost until her death on January 19, 1981.

First on the Rollins list of 10 anticipated publications was *A Proposal To Save The Shaker Community At Hancock, Massachusetts*. The next year *The Realities of Restoring The Shaker Community at Hancock, Massachusetts*, was published. Both helpful booklets were planned by them and were printed by Connecticut Printers, Inc.

Margaret Rollins had predicted that on opening day, July 2, 1961, the Village Bookstore would have some interesting material on sale, and it did. Originally, the store was located with the office in a room on the right as one entered the Brick Dwelling from the west. Here, Amy Bess Miller and Village secretary Eileen Carmon greeted visitors, sold tickets ($1.00), as well as books, offered the Guest Book to be signed, kept accounts, answered letters and conducted modest business affairs.

Dr. Andrews had completed his *History of The Hancock Shakers, 1780-1960* for opening day. This had been printed by Connecticut Printers, Inc. under Mrs. Rollins's direction. Also on sale were the following books by Dr. Andrews:

1. *The Community Industries of the Shakers*, New York State Museum, 1933
2. *Shaker Furniture*, Yale University Press, 1937
3. *The Gift to be Simple*, J.J. Augustin Publishers, New York, 1940
4. *The People Called Shakers*, Oxford University Press, 1953
5. A series of pamphlets:
   (a) *Organization of the 1st Communities*
   (b) *Principles and Practices*
   (c) *Early History. Persecutions*
   (d) *Their Mode of Worship*
   (e) *Industries & Craftsmanship*
   (f) *Their Religious Art*

These six pamphlets had originally appeared as articles in *The Berkshire Eagle*, following the announcement that the Shaker property was being purchased by a nonprofit organization and would become a village museum — or outdoor museum, as termed by museum professionals.

Marguerite F. Melcher, a friend of Margaret Rollins and author of *The Shaker Adventure*, arranged with her publisher to supply the Bookstore with her history, and William Henry Harrison, then director of Fruitlands at Harvard, Massachusetts, sent 20 copies of *Gleanings From Old Shaker Journals* by Clara Endicott Sears, published by Houghton-Mifflin in 1916. Mr. Harrison later served as a trustee of Shaker Community, Inc.

In addition, there were several colored postcards by Louis Frohman, who has since done many other views of the Village. These books with other related matter, particularly *200 Years of Berkshire County History*, a pictorial history, and several jars of Shaker Chutney sent by Eldress Emma B. King "to be sold to benefit the Village," made a modest but respectable sales offering.

Other publications envisioned by Margaret Rollins were:

1. *The Shakers and American Civilization* by Edward D. Andrews
2. *Some Shaker Symbols*
3. *The Gift of Song*
4. *The Children's Order*
5. *Shaker Iron and Tin Ware*
6. *Shaker Barns (A Study in Architecture)*
7. *Studies in Western Americana*
    (a) Journal of Issachar Bates
    (b) Journal of one year (1805-6 by Benjamin S. Youngs)
    (c) Mission to the Shawnee Indian
8. *A History of the Shakers* (based on Brother I.N. Young's MS 1856)
9. *A Bibliography of Shaker Literature*

Mrs. Rollins also proposed that certain books and pamphlets out of print, and for which there was still a continuing demand, be republished. These included *The Gift to be Simple: Songs, Dances and Rituals of the American Shakers* by Edward D. Andrews (New York, 1940), since reprinted by Dover, New York; *The Community Industries of the Shakers* (Albany, 1933), since reprinted by the Emporium Press, Charlestown, Mass. *The Order of Christmas* by Edward D. Andrews (Oxford University Press, New York, 1953), and *The Shaker Covenant* (from original MS 1795).

Mr. and Mrs. Rollins inspired the trustees to pursue an active program in publishing, as will be seen from the list of books, pamphlets, brochures and "keepsakes" produced by commercial process or at the Village Printing Office in the Hired Men's House. This useful little building, ingeniously arranged for many purposes, was restored in 1977 and dedicated to Carl and Margaret Rollins.

The first major original undertaking by the trustees' committee on publication was *The American Shakers: From Neo-Christianity to Presocialism* by Henri Desroche, translated from the French and edited by John K. Savacool of the French department at Williams College. It was published by the University of Massachusetts Press, Amherst, 1971. M. Desroche, who visited Hancock, made an important contribution in his socio-theological study of the Shakers' style of living, at a time in this present day of renewed experiments with communal ways of existence.

In line with the growing interest in Shaker recipes, *The Best of Shaker Cooking* by Amy Bess Miller and Persis W. Fuller, was published in 1970 by MacMillan, New York. In the introduction the authors state:

> Shaker cooking was more than just good plain food. Like Shaker architecture, furniture, and dress, it expressed genuine simplicity, excellence of quality, resourcefulness, and imagination... While some of their recipes may seem excessively rich... to us today, we must remember that the Shakers ate in moderation and thrived on a well-balanced diet. Their intelligent approach to food values and nutrition in general, to good housekeeping practices, to use of natural foods and the preparation of all dishes with loving care should touch and benefit us as it did so many thousands of the Believers whose legacy of perfection we inherit. They said, "Trifles make perfection, but perfection is no trifle."

The jacket cover was a photograph of a sunlit window ledge in the Great Kitchen at Hancock by the late Samuel Chamberlain of Marblehead, long a staunch friend of Hancock. All royalties were designated to go to the Village and the sale of two hard cover and three paperback editions have produced more than $60,000 to date. It is from this collection of 500 recipes that Shaker dishes are selected for meals in the Believer's Dining Room at the Village yearly during the first week in August. Walter Muir Whitehill, director of the Boston Athenaeum, another cherished friend of the Village, wrote a foreword, a charming and perceptive appreciation of the Shakers.

The Shaker Image, co-published by the Village and the New York Graphic Society, Greenwich, Connecticut, 1974, was a fitting commemoration of the arrival of the first Shakers in America just 200 years before, in 1774. This handsome book, showing the Believers at work and in their homes from 1850 to about 1920, was the best possible way to answer the natural curiosity of visitors coming to Hancock asking what the Shakers looked like.

Elmer R. "Ray" Pearson, trustee of Shaker Community, Inc., student of Shaker history for many years and associate professor of design at the Illinois Institute of Technology, had made it his special province to track down and preserve every snapshot, every daguerreotype, every studio portrait or group portrait of the Shakers he could unearth as an expert photographer and technician. He rephotographed everything he found and, what was of great historical significance, identified the individuals in the photographs. His expertise insured that the best possible reproductions were obtained of old and rare photographs.

Julia Neal, an authority on Shaker history and founding trustee of Shakertown, South Union, an original Shaker settlement, now restored and opened to the public near Bowling Green, Kentucky, furnished the text and history of the sect in both East and Midwest communities during their 200 years on this continent. The late Walter Whitehill wrote the preface and aptly drew the parallel between the restoration of an eastern Massachusetts Shaker Village with Hancock Shaker Village in the western part of the state:

> More than fifty years ago, when I was in my teens, I first heard of the Shakers when my mother bought a copy of *Gleanings From Old Shaker Journals*, which had been compiled by Miss Clara Endicott Sears and published by Houghton Mifflin Company in 1916. Miss Sears, who was born in 1863 and died in 1960, was a Boston lady of property and leisure who had built for herself a house on the crest of Prospect Hill in Harvard, Massachusetts, from which one could look across the Nashaway Valley toward Mount Wachusett. Although she was as unencumbered by formal education as most Boston ladies of her generation, Miss Sears had compensating gifts of imagination and energy that led her not only to appreciate the natural beauty and historical implications of her surroundings, but also to do something positive and constructive about them. It was inevitable that Miss Sears should be attracted to the dwindling membership of the Shaker Community established in 1793 within the town of Harvard. In the twentieth century, its numbers steadily shrank, and the community was dissolved in 1918. Miss Sears often visited the last of the Shaker eldresses, and through their friendship gained access to the records from which she compiled *Gleanings From Old Shaker Journals*. When the community came to an end she bought from the deserted Shaker Village the 1794 wooden office and moved it to her own property, resettling it on the hill a little above Fruitlands. This building was opened to exhibit a collection that she had formed illustrative of Shaker life and industries, as memorial to the extinct community.

John Ott and Amy Bess Miller wrote the captions to the photographs in *The Shaker Image*. So much new material has been collected since this was published that a sequel is being contemplated by the Village.

In 1976, *Shaker Herbs: A History and a Compendium* by Amy Bess Miller was published by Clarkson N. Potter, New York. It was illustrated with watercolor drawings of herbs by Sister Cora Helena Sarle, done in 1886 and 1887 under the direction of Elder Henry Clay Blinn, of Canterbury, New Hampshire, who wrote the plant descriptions. These drawings were loaned by the Village's old friend, Charles Thompson, curator at Shaker Village, Canterbury, New Hampshire. They are the same annotated drawings which were used as teaching devices to help Shaker schoolchildren memorize their native plants. This history of medicinal herbs gives credence to the Shaker adage that the truly useful is always the truly beautiful. The royalties from this book have also gone to support the Village.

In March of 1980, *Shaker Textile Arts* by Beverly Gordon was published by the University Press of New England in cooperation with the Merrimack Valley Textile Museum and Shaker Community, Inc. It was reissued in paperback in 1982. A carefully researched and well-illustrated book, it describes the kinds of textiles the Shakers used, how they were produced, and their cultural and economic importance to the communities.

Soon to be published is a sociological study of the Shakers by Hancock research assistant Priscilla Brewer. In 1984 *A Book of Shaker Furniture* will be published by the University Press of New England.

This comprehensive history, fully illustrated, covers the Shakers' most important craft. It includes essays by Mary Julia Neal, Robert F.W. Meader, Theodore E. Johnson, Sister Mildred Barker, Katherine Finkelpearl, Elmer R. Pierson, Dorothy Filley, John Scherer, June Sprigg, Robert Emlen, Aviva Baal-Teshuva, Elaine Piraino-Holevoet, Bayard Underwood and Ed Nickels.

No publication can be of more importance to visitors to the Village than John Ott's *Hancock Shaker Village, a Guidebook and History*. Research for this book began soon after Ott joined the Village staff, first as its curator in 1970 and after 1972 as its director. Data uncovered became the material for the thesis of his master of arts degree in American History Museum Training awarded by the State University of New York at Oneonta and the New York State Historical Association at Cooperstown. While its writing was stimulated by a professional advancement, it was truly a labor of love. It also has the discipline of a work which had to meet the test of accuracy and original research.

The trustees are proud of the growing list of books published with the assistance of Hancock Shaker Village. A Shaker tradition is perpetuated and in 20 years' time, important research has been accomplished. To date, royalties from all publications have returned more than $80,000 to the revolving publications fund.

In addition to the books and pamphlets concerned with Shakerism bearing the imprimatur of Hancock Shaker Village, numerous magazine articles have appeared about the Hancock restoration. These include *The Magazine ANTIQUES, House & Garden, House Beautiful, The Smithsonian, American Heritage Society's Americana, Women's Day, Family Circle, Better Homes & Gardens, Time, Leisure, Yankee Magazine* and *Early American Heritage*.

The English periodical, *Country Life*, in 1974 commemorated the bicentenary of the arrival of the Shakers in America in a series of three articles on the life and contributions of the Shakers. The articles were written by John Conforth, who visited Hancock while doing his research. The numerous photographs were of high quality.

Bales of newspaper feature articles, of course, have appeared from coast to coast with pleasing regularity, especially a culinary salute to Shaker cookery by Craig Claiborne, the *New York Times*'s leading food writer. Perhaps no publication, however, evoked such satisfaction as the announcement in *Historic Preservation*, the quarterly of the National Trust for Historic Preservation, Vol. 13, No. 2, 1961, that the Village had opened to the public. The announcement showed an aerial view of the community.

From the beginning of the restoration, the Village needed exposure in order to be known. Paid attendance is an important item in its budget and it was through editors, reporters, feature writers and television exposure that word of the Village spread, always greatly appreciated by Hancock trustees.

The project has been blessed, literally, with the sympathetic understanding of gifted writers who have for 22 years told the story of Hancock and its needs. To these the enterprise owes the attendance of its visitors and the financial support of those whose presence at special events have made the Village prosper.

In recent years Lili Ott, wife of the director, performed a task the Village is totally dependent upon for exposure. It is called publicity, but a more descriptive word might be survival for it is imperative that word of the Village, its activities and its attractions reach as far and wide as possible. Lili sent our message far and wide. She also added the writing of promotional ads to her regular dispatches.

Meeting House at Shirley in 1960, before being moved to Hancock.

In 1963, the Village opened its first herb garden.

PROFESSIONAL PERSONNEL AND STAFF

There is a Shaker song titled, "Precept And Line," which goes "Precept on precept and line upon line, Mother has trod, Yea, straight and clear straightness, the pure way of God." According to Edward D. Andrews in *The Gift To Be Simple: Songs, Dances and Rituals of the American Shakers*, which he published in 1940, the song was sung slowly and deliberately as the worshipers placed one foot before the other in "the narrow path."

When the founding members of the new corporation, which would eventually purchase and restore Hancock Shaker Village, decided upon their course, they were led and encouraged by Dr. and Mrs. Andrews. These two had been scholar-collectors of Shaker history and artifacts since the 1920s, and gave unstintedly of their time and expertise in the organization of the operation.

Mark Van Doren, a friend of the Andrewses and a friend of many of the trustees of Shaker Community, Inc., wrote a memorial tribute to Dr. Andrews in 1964:

> The word authority, often loosely used to mean one who knows more than most people do about some subject, regains its dignity as soon as we consider Edward Deming Andrews. He knew more about the Shakers than anyone ever has, and I am quite certain that his knowledge of them will never be surpassed. He knew about them; he knew of them; he knew them. His interest in them was many-sided, and indeed was inexhaustible. Not merely their furniture, though that may have been his chief concern, but their songs, their dances, their craftsmanship, their herbs, their drawings, their paintings, their chothes, their manners, their customs, and finally — crown of all — their religion drew out of him a scholarship so dedicated that for purity, for precision, and for completeness it stands alone in our time. He knew the Shakers in this wonderful way because he loved them: not sentimentally, not nostalgically, but with an abiding respect for the ideas their entire life expressed. And he knew how to write of what he so perfectly understood. To enter a room full of Shaker furniture is a unique experience; it takes the breath. But to read one of his books is, to the extent that such a thing now is possible, to inhabit that room.

It was therefore Dr. and Mrs. Andrews who provided the early guidance and historical direction which was, like the song, "Straight and Clear," and as the song was sung slowly and deliberately as the worshipers placed one foot before the other in "the narrow path," so too at Hancock the progress was slow and deliberate. This conduct of action so well established then in 1959-1960 has been a guiding rule ever since and one that has averted costly mistakes.

Mrs. Andrews was her husband's able assistant and colleague. She was also an intrepid volunteer at the Village in receiving visitors and talking about the Shakers. It was interesting to hear from one who had personal knowledge of the Shakers over many years. As rooms in the Sisters' Shop, the Dwelling House and the Ministry Wash House were restored, furniture and household and shop accessories form the Andrews collection were installed, Mrs. Andrews had a large and important part in the correct arrangements, which were beautiful because they were simple, simplicity being one of the most pervasive of Shaker virtues.

Thomas Merton, writing from the Abbey of Gethsemani Trappist, in Kentucky, in 1964 after Dr. Andrews's death said:

> There is no question that his vocation was to keep alive the Shaker spirit in its purity and mediate that to the rest of us. I feel personally very much in debt to him for this. I realize more and more the vital importance of the Shaker "gift of simplicity" which is a true American

charism; alas, not as fully appreciated as it should be.

Attendance at the Village started off briskly in July 1961, and continued until closing day early in October. Dr. Andrews, functioning as curator, established his office in the Ministry dining room near the center of the Brick Dwelling where he could easily meet visitors. In addition to Philip Clark, buildings and grounds superintendent, the staff consisted of Clark's assistants, Leo Lemieux and Walter Pictrowski and for part-time help, C.E. Mackie. Nancy Ferris, a Smith College senior, was tour hostess and in charge of the Sisters' Shop. There were four guides who did everything: cleaning, conducting tours, and policing the grounds and parking area. They were Andrew W. Fuller, Norman O. McClintock, Mark C. Miller and Alfred C. Symonds III, head guide.

As the second season approached in 1962, several trustees felt the need for a director and administrator. Dr. Andrews preferred to remain Village curator, occupying his office in the Brick Dwelling when the Village was open during the summer and fall. He was busy other times of the year lecturing, meeting with students, writing and consulting on the overall program and continuous restoration. He was with the Village as curator until June of 1962, when he retired.

The growing attendance could be attributed to the visitors and supporters whose interest in Shaker history was accelerating faster perhaps than had been anticipated, and it was certain their numbers would continue to increase. The work in all phases of Village management and restoration was now beyond normal expectations.

Emphasizing the need for coordination, a committee of the board undertook to look for a director. After several months of search, Wilbur H. Glover was offered the position. At that time Dr. Glover was director of the Buffalo and Erie County Historical Society, where he had been for 10 years. He also served as a city and county historian. The committee had canvassed the field extensively, screening more than 15 candidates.

Dr. Glover was chosen because of his reputation as an excellent scholar and good administrator, widely known in the fields of historical research, museum operation and historical society administration. Dr. Glover, 55, was a graduate of Milton (Wisconsin) College and received his master's and doctor's degrees from the University of Wisconsin, where he also taught from 1931 to 1945, and for the next two years was a research associate there.

Mrs. Edgar B. Stern, a trustee, offered to underwrite Dr. Glover's salary for two years so that this administrative cost would not further burden the budget. One of Dr. Glover's first duties was to work with Terry Hallock and Francis Vosburgh, of Richmond, in completing work as previously mentioned on a Reception Center for visitors.

Under Dr. Glover's direction the Village's business in every area continued to increase as did the attendance. The director was an able and enthusiastic speaker, each month filling several engagements which helped publicize the Village. He also accelerated one of the most laborious of duties, that of cataloging the growing collections.

Soon it became apparent to the trustees that a vigorous fund-raising campaign was a necessity. The Friends of Hancock Shaker Village had been organized in the spring of 1965 and many in this new group were eager to be a part of Village planning and other activities to assist the trustees. This was the second adjunct to the Village operation, the first being the Shaker Kitchen Sisters, organized in 1964. The rapidly deteriorating state of the Round Stone Barn indicated that a drive for funds to stabilize it pending complete restoration was the No. 1 priority.

Unfortunately, although he had been a strong supporter of a campaign, Wilber Glover felt that his health would limit his activities in this field. He submitted his resignation in 1964, leaving the Village in the able and professional hands of Miss Henrietta Granville of New York, who had been working with him on the installation of recently acquired collections of furniture and artifacts. She was assisted by Alan Thielker of Interlaken, Massachusetts, who was appointed acting curator upon Dr. Glover's resignation.

Walter Muir Whitehill, historian and director of the Boston Athenaeum, telephoned during the summer of 1965 to say that Eugene Merrick

Dodd, a young Harvard-trained architectural historian, had recently returned to the Boston area from California, where he had been assistant professor in the School of Architecture at the University of California at Berkeley. He had also been a consultant in architectural history for several San Francisco architects. Dr. Whitehill suggested that Dodd be interviewed to see if he might fit the needs of the Village as its curator.

Dr. Dodd was well qualified. After receiving his bachelor's degree from Harvard in 1956, he received his master's at the Courtauld Institute of the University of London, where he also obtained his doctorate. While at Harvard he was assistant librarian at Eliot House for three years and after graduating he was curatorial assistant for the drawings collection at the Fogg Museum of Art. At Harvard, in addition to being art editor and then president of a literary publication, the *Advocate*, he was secretary of the Harvard Dramatic Club.

In October of 1965 the trustees elected Dr. Dodd to fill the position of curator, the post he served with distinction until he resigned in 1970 to complete a book on Shaker design, for Clarkson Potter, Inc. One of his most useful legacies is the semiannual newsletter to the Friends which he launched and edited. This had the immense value of informing supporters of Village events, past, present, and future and of keeping them aware of the needs and aspirations of the Village. In writing this history it has been valuable in recalling hundreds of activities, acquisitions, events and newly researched Shaker material. Dr. Dodd wrote with skill and flavor, and was sought after by several publications for articles dealing with the Shakers. His most prestigious contribuiton was his article for *The Magazine ANTIQUES* issue of October, 1970, titled "Functionalism in Shaker Crafts."

Gene Dodd, a bachelor, lived on the third floor of the Brick Dwelling, and was as indefatigable in lecturing about the Village as he was concerned with some of the most important phases of restoration. During his five years as curator, the Ministry Shop and the Laundry and Machine Shop were wholly restored and furnished. The Mary Earle Gould Collection of 1,200 pieces of early American wooden, iron and tinware items, many of them Shaker made, came to the Village to be integrated into the existing collections or viewed in a comparative sense.

The largest and most spectacular project, restoration of the Round Stone Barn, took place while Dr. Dodd was curator. His pamphlet on the Barn is a collector's item. He also directed the Village's staff in preparing a Shaker exhibition which was shipped to Japan for the United States Pavilion at Expo '70. Those are some of the highlights of his activities during the five years he was at the Village.

John Harlow Ott joined the Village staff as curator following Dr. Dodd's resignation in the fall of 1970. Ott was soon to receive his M.A. degree from the American Museum Training Program at Cooperstown, which is administered by the State University of New York at Oneonta. Following his course of academic studies, he enlisted in the U.S. Army as an engineering maintenance officer and spent one year in Vietnam. A short time after his discharge he came to Hancock, where he was soon dubbed "Mr. Clean" by his fellow workers as he took to heart the Shaker saying, "A place for everything and everything in its place." It was his ambition, he said, to give visitors more of what he called "the feel, and even the smells," of the Shaker life, to better reflect the character and the innovative spirit of the Shakers.

A year later the trustees appointed John Ott director. There is no segment of the Village operation which did not benefit from his scrutiny. His leadership and resourcefulness, his energy and foresight demonstrated how to build on the labors of the past.

In 1983, after more than 12 years as Village director, Ott resigned to become director of the Atlanta (Georgia) Historical Society. The Trustees, after interviewing many candidates for the director's position, found a well qualified successor to Ott right at the Village itself: He is Jerry V. Grant, who has worked at Hancock in various capacities since he joined the staff in 1978, most recently as administrative coordinator after the Ott family's departure for Atlanta.

Under John Ott's leadership, impressive progress was made in restoring buildings, farmlands and forests at the community. Perhaps the most important accomplishment under his direction was the establishment of Shaker Community

Top, John H. Ott, former director; center, Jerry V. Grant, present director; bottom, June Sprigg, former curator.

Industries in the 1910 Barn, restored especially for this endeavor.

While involved in research for restoration, Ott uncovered data which became the material for the thesis for his Master of Arts Degree in American Museum History Training, awarded by the State University of New York at Oneonta and the New York State Historical Association at Cooperstown. In 1976, this manuscript became a guidebook and history of the Village.

Under Ott's direction a professional staff developed. Still few in number, they have nevertheless put on imaginative workshops, programs for school and tour groups, edited or written articles and full-length books, designed and installed a variety of exhibitions, both at the Village and in Boston, New York City and at the University of Connecticut at Storrs. These accomplishments are only a fraction of their activities outside their involvement in the daily obligation of maintaining, protecting, and interpreting a large and growing collection housed in 20 buildings.

With the opening of each additional shop and dwelling, the staff has become involved in the introduction of such activities as cabinetmaking, forging, tin-smithing, herb culture, basketry, broom and box making, chair taping, and weaving for demonstration and sale. There are also lectures to give and a continuing publications program to oversee.

An important step forward in the spring of 1977 was the addition of June Sprigg to the Village as curator. John Ott had fulfilled these duties as well as those of director since 1971. As these responsibilities increased with the growth of the Village and its collections, the trustees felt it necessary and prudent to add a curator to the staff.

June Sprigg received a bachelor of arts degree in 1974 from Lafayette College and a master of arts from the Winterthur Program at the University of Delaware in 1977. Before that, she had lived for several months with the Shaker family at Canterbury while writing and illustrating her book, "By Shaker Hands" (a must for all Shaker enthusiasts), published by Alfred Knopf in 1976.

She therefore came to Hancock with a love for the Shakers and a background of their history which is apparent in her knowledgeable lectures and her writing. Her first big assignment was to design and prepare a major exhibition held at the University of Connecticut's Benton Museum at Storrs in the spring of 1978: "Simple Gifts: Hands to Work and Hearts to God."

On May 31, 1981, June Sprigg was awarded an honorary doctorate of letters from her alma mater, Lafayette College in Easton, Pennsylvania, and was the commencement speaker. She spoke on the need for tolerance and on the fact that our society cannot afford the attitudes toward women and minorities prevalent 150 years ago when the college was founded.

June Sprigg resigned in the spring of 1983 and has been succeeded as curator of collections by Thomas F. Harrington, a newcomer to the Village.

In reality, the entire Village exists to educate, for as soon as a visitor enters, he is surrounded in one way or another with the story of the Hancock Shakers and gradually, but in less detail, he hears about the families of 17 other Shaker communities in the United States dating from 1787, two of which are still lived in and managed by the Shakers.

In the hall of the Visitors' Center there are pictures, maps and examples of furniture made at Hancock; a flyer detailing the 20 buildings in the Village is given out. But that is only the beginning. There are guides to lead groups on tour; there are movies and a slide talk to be sure that all aspects of Shaker life are covered. Of the thousands who come to Hancock each summer, some may seek a quiet place. The quiet places at the Village may be the trails blazed by the Boy Scouts up the north slope opposite the Village, or the meadows overlooking the Village from the west, which are fragrant with wild thyme, pleasant picnic spots in the summer and undisturbed in the winter for cross-country skiing and snowshoeing.

The well-being of the visitor, his exposure to the Shaker story, and to the life the Believers led at Hancock is the responsibility of the curator of education, who also trains the guides to act as interpreters and as it has been said, "To oil the doorways to history." The first person to hold this important position was Cheryl Anderson. She inaugurated "An Evening with the Shakers"

At top, a demonstration in tinsmithing.

Below, Loranne Block at the spinning wheel.

A cooking demonstration, top, in the kitchen of the 1830 Brick Dwelling.

Blacksmithing in the Tan House.

Professional Personnel and Staff / 151

A fall weekend at the Village, especially for children.

152 / Hancock Shaker Village

Professional Personnel and Staff / 153

*At top, seating a Shaker chair.
And below, stone-cutting on a craft weekend.*

*At left, Village trustee John Monroe working
in the Community Industries program.*

and directed it for five years, only one of her many contributions.

It is not possible to list all the guides and interpreters who have been a part of the education department. Roughly, more than 250 have made important contributions to the Village during the recent decades.

On a blackboard for all to see are listed the special events of the day: A demonstration of cooking in the Great Kitchen in the Brick Dwelling; weaving to be observed in the Sisters' Shop where the shuttle may be passed from the guide to a visitor "to get the feel"; a tinsmith in the Brethren's Shop will demonstrate and answer questions, while in the next room to him, "fingers" of oval boxes are painstakingly "wrapped around."

There is no end of variety in a day at Hancock, which often ends with the singing of Shaker songs, and again the visitor is urged to join in.

The Village has been fortunate in having some very talented and dedicated interpreters and curators in this essential program. Many times it is the people trained by this department who are the only members of the staff to come in contact with the visitor, and it is with pride that their responsibility is recognized here.

It is natural to be puzzled and curious about those who devote themselves to a religious cause, and in the case of the Shakers, to celibacy as well. Spiritual motivations seem all the more difficult to grasp. It is the curator of education who must arrive at an understandable description and interpretation of Shaker tenets and philosophy.

Sisters Aida Elam and Miriam Wall of the Canterbury Shakers wrote *A Brief History of the Education and Recreation of the Shakers*, and they state simply: "A Community of Shakers is a religious body, or group of people living together for the promotion of the spiritual interests of each other. Its government is through rules, consistent with reason, and the teachings of Jesus Christ."

The visitor must also be shown that the Shakers, unlike most utopian societies, had the knack of succeeding in practically all that they undertook. The societies not only were self-supporting but were models of enterprise, efficiency, ingenuity, sound business practice and fair dealing. There is so much to tell at Hancock; for instance, all the inventions credited to the Shakers: the circular saw, the rotary or disc harrow, the sidehill plow, the threshing machine, the flat broom, the clothespin, a machine for making tongue-in-groove boards, and an improved washing machine for commercial and institutional use.

John Kouwenhoven said: "The Shakers had no fear of the machine." This is apparent when the guides point out the vast collection of machines and devices used by the original craftsmen and farmers at Hancock.

After a lengthy review of more than 90 applicants, Director Ott was fortunate in finding a capable and experienced new curator of education in Roma Hansis. She had a B.A. from Beloit College, an M.A. in history from Claremont (California) Graduate School, where she also completed her doctoral work. She taught college-level history and social studies at Mount Greylock Regional High School in Williamstown, Massachusetts. She also had worked with the Village in a joint program with Mount Greylock, the Village and the Massachusetts Educational Collaborative. Susan Markham succeed Roma Hansis as curator of education in 1982.

In every small organization there is a nice feeling that everyone is familiar with all aspects of the work, but there has to be a linchpin and at Hancock it is Beverly Hamilton, the registrar. She works out the weekly schedules, posts the daily events, assists the director and other members of the staff and keeps up a continuous dialogue with the Lunch Shop, the office staff and the volunteers. She is also responsible for the monthly calendar issued to all periodicals.

There has always been concern at the Village for feeding the visitors. At first a lunch counter was located in the 1950 Shaker garage west of the Dwelling where Bob McCain made his famous Shaker Burgers. A larger lunch shop was included in plans for the Visitors' Center when summer and fall attendance exceeded 40,000. Open from 11 to 3 it can seat 40 at one time at Shaker tables and chairs and has been operated first by Francis Duval and her family and for the past five years by Pat and Bonnie Mele and members of their family.

The Meles also provide Shaker lunches by

advance reservation only but the thousands who have been refreshed with Bonnie's homemade soups, a variety of sandwiches made to individual order and homemade desserts go away praising "Shaker" food. Pat Mele as manager is sure to please every weary traveler, young or old.

Bonnie also supplies the Good Room with Shaker breads, cookies and cakes.

It has been estimated, conservatively, by a friend with a slide rule and a long memory, that the volunteers at Hancock over a period of 20 years have contributed, had they been paid, the equivalent of more than $300,000. This may well be conservative when the time of the trustees at the meetings, and the staff and other employees devote to special events outside of working hours, is calculated.

Seven days a week for six months when the Village is open to the public, there are volunteers in charge of, or assisting in the Bookstore, the Good Room, the Herb Shop and the Fancy Goods Shop in the Trustees' Office. When large groups are expected and the staff is shorthanded, they respond. When there are special events in Boston or New York such as the recent exhibition and reception after the Ellis Memorial Show in Boston or the reception at the Hirschl & Adler Art Galleries in New York and the exhibition for a month which followed, our Friends gave hours of their time. When meetings are arranged in areas outside the Village in larger communities to bring Village supporters up to date, it is the volunteers who arrange and sponsor these events.

Shaker Community, Inc., the parent organization of Hancock Shaker Village, has offered the opportunity to many men, women and children to develop every form of ability, for every grade of their genius, and hundreds have taken advantage of this for the overall good of the Village.

The Village has been fortunate in having competent office management.

Eileen Carmon served as executive secretary from 1960 until 1967. She was succeeded by Mary Drury and at her sudden death in 1968, Mrs. Carmon returned until 1972 and was succeeded by Phyllis Rubenstein, who directed a growing office staff for nine years until her retirement in 1981.

Beverly Hamilton, the registrar of the Village, gives a spinning lesson.

Mrs. Rubenstein had been a summer resident of New Lebanon, New York, but in 1972 had decided to live there permanently in the house she built following the death of her husband.

For nine years she demonstrated how an office could be run with professional skill and little additional help, finding ways of achieving growth with an eye on the budget. Her personal concern for the well-being of the Village is responsible in large measure for the good management procedures she instituted.

These stalwarts and their successors deserve a chapter of their own which would include the Village maintenance staff headed by Walter Pictrowski, a veteran of 22 years. Walter knows where everything is, how to get at it in the case of buried pipes, how to make a secondhand truck perform like a new one, how to decorate the Village with Christmas trees and wreathes and himself as Santa Claus for the Annual Holiday Sale.

Charles Perego joined the permanent restoration staff at the Village in 1970 and made a significant contribution until his death on October 6, 1972, at the age of 72. This is brief perhaps, in the recent history of the Village, but it is long in what he accomplished in that short period.

Three hundred feet of triple-rail white fencing, united by three 10-foot gates, all handmade, were his earliest work. During the winter months, Perego renewed floors, doors and walls, built shelving in the storage rooms, strengthened skylights and removed partitions to expose the beautiful built-in storage cabinets on the fourth floor of the Brick Dwelling. There was not an area which was not enhanced by his work.

All the carpentry involved in setting up the displays in "The Shaker Farmer's Year" in the east ell of the Round Barn was his work. The nearby Ice House, restored and opened in 1967, was perhaps his proudest accomplishment.

One is amazed to count up the projects Perego finished in 24 months. He remodeled the small Shaker-built garage west of the Brick Dwelling in the spring to be the Guide's House and built the two long boardwalks which lead to the new Visitors' Center and from it to the herb garden. Pine cabinets and shelves in the three offices at the Center and along the 16-foot wall in the Bookstore are also a reminder that no job was ever too big or too small for him.

When restoration was started on the Tan House, Perego was a member of the team and particularly happy because he was working with Francis Conroy, whose career as a master mason he helped further many years earlier when Perego was superintendent for the contracting and engineering firm of Carroll, Verge & Whipple. His friends at Hancock Shaker Village planted an oak tree in the Village's Tree of Life Arboretum in his memory. Mrs. Perego gave all of her husband's tools to the Village to be used in the Village crafts shops, certainly a great memorial to his skills.

William Senseney, the Village blacksmith.

THE FUTURE OF THE CITY OF PEACE

Thousands of visitors — over 800,000 during the months when the Village is open to visitors — have come to Hancock since 1960. This does not include volunteers, trustees, friends, council members and distinguished groups whose visits in and out of season would bring the figure well over a million.

They have followed restoration with avid curiosity. They have encouraged and supported Hancock Shaker Village financially. They have given artifacts and distinguished pieces of Shaker furniture to enlarge the collections. As volunteers, they have contributed hours of productive and faithful service.

Each spring, we are asked what has been done during the preceding winter: what is new, and what there is still to do. This concluding chapter answers the last question — but only in part. The excitement of being involved in continuing restoration, replanting, and uncovering and documenting new areas will be as stimulating as it was for those who were privileged to participate in the initial restoration more than 20 years ago.

> There is no failure except in no longer trying. There is no defeat except from within: no really unsurmountable barrier save our own inherent weakness of purpose.

These words of Sister Amelia J. Carver of the Shaker Village at Mount Lebanon were wise and cautious in 1889. They were directed toward her community, still striving to grow and to sustain a strong membership. Her words have meaning for us today, exhorting us to continue the work which has started so well but is not yet finished.

The renewal of Hancock Shaker Village began in 1960 with dedication and purpose. Young friends, young trustees and young staff are dedicating themselves to perpetuate a tradition of "harmonious development" which was an integral part of the Shaker tradition.

Early in Hancock's Shaker history, Father James Whitaker urged a neighborhood farm family, "When you have done all you can towards seeding your land for the present season, set yourselves faithfully to put your whole place in order." This commitment to order was endorsed by the trustees when they first undertook to restore the Village at Hancock in 1960.

In a sense, the season of physical restoration now nears its end as a season of commitment to the "whole place" begins.

For Hancock, the whole place involves not only the physical appearance of the Village, but as complete and vital a record as possible of life within the Village. For almost two centuries, this life and the life of a young nation ran together; the record of one would be incomplete without the record of the other.

In 1981, the trustees of the Village committed themselves to a capital fund drive with a twofold purpose: to finance the development of certain projects important to the "whole place" of the Village, and to create an endowment for perpetuation of the work undertaken since restoration began more than two decades ago. The goal for the drive is two million dollars.

And we are well under way. A long-range planning committe, working with the Village staff, has developed a list of priority projects which they feel must be seen to completion if Hancock is to become a whole Village.

Some involve bricks and mortar.

Others are concerned with the propagation of trees and plants, and with re-establishing the animals who once made the Hancock land productive for the Shakers.

Still others seek to document the way of life which the Village will recreate for its visitors.

The Farm Program

When Father James Whitaker urged Josiah Talcott to "get thy farm in readiness," he was talking about the current agricultural season, and about larger issues such as survival and the symbolic importance of an orderly farm in the chaotic world of the late 18th century. When the Shakers first put down roots in Hancock, they were surrounded by a New England which had recently become independent and was, to a large extent, ungoverned.

Only a few years before the establishment of the settlements at Hancock and Mount Lebanon, Berkshire neighbors of the Shakers had participated in a bloody insurgence against what was essentially starvation. The skirmishing of Shays' Rebellion, shortly after the American Revolution, must have added a sense of urgency to springtime tillage at Hancock: Food was a requisite to survival, and without money (and there was none) food could not be bought. It had to be grown.

Recreation of a Shaker agricultural program thus becomes basic to the restoration of the Hancock community as a whole. Without the animals, crops and vegetables grown by the Shakers, the Village is not complete. To remedy this, the trustees and the Village director have developed a farm program which will demonstrate Shaker farming techniques and provide sustenance to the Village as well.

The 1946 dairy wing extension to the southeast of the Round Stone Barn has been renovated as a general livestock facility to house dairy cattle, horses, sheep and poultry. Draft horses and possibly teams of oxen once again will work the lands surrounding the Village. Original breeds of cattle such as Durhams, Holderness and Shorthorns, sheep (Southdowns, Cotswolds and Leicester), and poultry (white and brown Leghorns, grey Darkings and Plymouth Rocks) will fill the barn. Even a pair of Berkshire hogs or a MacKoy or two might be found.

Farming all of Hancock's productive acreage lies beyond the intentions and capacities of the Village. But visitors — children especially — will be able to see demonstrations of how the Shakers used the land with equipment then available, and how they looked after the animals which were essential to their survival.

A Shaker brother spent much of his time in the fields or in the barns; he and many of his sisters were also occupied with garden work.

Initially, they grew vegetables and fruits to feed themselves. As the gardens and orchards expanded, there was surplus — surplus to feed many hungry visitors, and to sell to the World. Almost at the outset of the Shaker experience, there were garden seeds to peddle, seeds of a quality which made Shaker husbandry famous in America and elsewhere.

The gardens at Hancock, on the north side of Route 20, are being re-established. They cannot, however, simply be replanted. Decades of hybridizing separate us from plant varieties which the Shaker seed industry made famous. Re-discovering the strains which the Shakers used more than a century ago is an important part of the agricultural research at the Village — a goal shared, incidentally, with many home gardeners who are finding that today's hybrid cannot compete with its ancestor in taste, nourishment or hardiness. Hancock can once again grow the mangel-beet, the marrow-fat pea, the mammoth lettuce and other vegetables we would eat today if we had access to them. Rediscovering and reintroducing neglected garden varieties becomes a challenge which Hancock can meet.

"It was strongly impressed upon us," wrote a Shaker sister in the mid-19th century, "that a rose was useful, not ornamental." Just as they cultivated the rose for medicinal and culinary purposes, the Shakers grew an enormous variety of herbs for the good that could be extracted from them. At Hancock, the present half-acre herb garden is a beginning toward reconstitution of what was once a flourishing medicinal garden and industry. For every variety already established, there are ten others at least which must be grown in quantity before the herb garden can truly be called a Shaker garden.

New England is famous — justly — for its maple products, and the Shakers at Hancock early took advantage of an extensive "sugar bush" on the property they acquired. Untapped in recent years, these maples should be brought back into production, not only because of the Village's commitment to productive agriculture, but also as a wintertime learning experience for visitors.

Keeping bees is a special art; not all Shaker communities took on this occupation. Hancock, however, did. Two hives are now producing honey for the Sisters' Good Room but more are needed to keep natural honey stocked on the shelves.

The Energy Program

A museum in New England, particularly if it encompasses a whole village, inevitably faces a choice: It limits its public activity to the warm months, or it undertakes an enormous financial commitment to keep its buildings habitable year-round. At Hancock, the trustees have lived with a compromise for the last two decades. The Village is open on a total basis from the end of May through the end of October. Thereafter, certain buildings are kept open and are available for special wintertime events and for year-long operation of the Community Industries Program.

An energy survey early in 1982 convinced the trustees that a substantial investment should be made to winterize more of the buildings — both to economize on fuel and power costs and to make possible a broader range of public activity during the cold months.

To some extent, this investment will make possible a greater utilization of the energy resources mobilized by the Hancock Shakers themselves. Water power, for example, exists in potential abundance, and can be used to drive many of the machines which were once used at the Village. Whether it can produce electricity for Village power remains to be explored.

Shaker buildings were well constructed but uninsulated. Every room of any size had its own wood-burning stove, so that the Village's inhabitants did not go cold in winter. The trustees face a different problem today: First, there are not enough Village residents to keep hundreds of fires stoked throughout the community; second, the priceless collections which the Village has acquired cannot be exposed to unnecessary fire hazards. Therefore, the trustees and director plan to insulate those buildings which are essential to an expanded winter program, and to modernize their heating plants.

The Other Families

So far, Hancock Shaker Village has concentrated its efforts at restoration of the Church Family site. There were, however, five other Shaker Families closely associated with the community at Hancock. In the first half of the 19th century, the West, East, North, South and Second Families were established as adjuncts to the central Church Family. In some instances, these families committed themselves to agrarian and industrial activity which was separate from, though complementary to, work done directly under supervision of the Church Family.

The West Family, for example, exploited mineral rights to land under its control. The North Family for some years operated a substantial carding and fulling mill. With the decline in society membership in the later 1800s, these subsidiary families were dissolved, one by one, and their remaining members gathered into the central Church Family. The buildings in which they lived and which housed their industries were either moved to the area occupied by the Church Family, sold to neighbors, or destroyed by fire.

Above ground, little remains to remind one of the activity of the families which surrounded the Church Family locus. However, preliminary surface exploration tells us beyond doubt that there is much to be learned about these families, and about the operation of the community as a whole, literally by digging up the evidence, through a program of carefully supervised archaeological research.

For example, the water system; north of the various family settlements there is a substantial water supply which the Shakers used to their advantage from the outset. Springs on Mount Sinai and its surrounding elevations were tapped, reservoirs built, and lines buried to supply water by gravity not only for use of village inhabitants but also as a source of industrial power. Some of these water lines still function and are used by the Village today. Others must be rediscovered and put back in working order. The trustees' historical interest in reactivating these systems is fortified by a further urgency: Water, here as everywhere, is a precious natural resource, vital to people and to growing food.

And what of the industries which once flourished on the acres which surround Hancock Village? The foundations of mills, storage buildings and dwellings are there to be explored. With an active history that spans so much of this country's early life as an independent nation, Hancock's acres offer a unique opportunity for archaeological research and reconstruction.

Subject to funding, Rensselaer Polytechnic Institute and Hancock Shaker Village have agreed to launch an archaeological investigation which can, if successful, restore two dams and revitalize the water systems which the Shakers used.

Research and Publications

The Village library, as presently constituted, consists of some 2,500 bound volumes by and about the Shakers, and in addition ancillary works on subjects such as agriculture, industry, state and local history. There are maps, drawings, photographs of Hancock and other Shaker communities, bound manuscripts which are the basis for Shaker research.

Also in the archives on microfilm and microfiche are the collections of the Western Reserve Historical Society, without doubt the greatest repository of Shakeriana in the world. The Hancock library also has acquired on microfilm the Shaker material of the New York State Library. No museum can continue to operate today without a research library and modern facilities; ours forms a fine background for present activities at the City of Peace.

We are anxious to round out our microfilm collection by acquiring copies of material at the Library of Congress in Washington. There is also an extensive cataloguing project under way which must be completed.

Hancock Shaker Village has from the outset recognized its responsibility toward students of Shaker life by making its collections and facilities available to scholars. In addition to keeping in print valuable reference works, the trustees have participated in financing or co-publishing newly completed studies. Several Hancock staff members, as detailed in the chapter on publications, have published works about the Shakers.

Through grants-in-aid to scholars, and through direct participation in publishing ventures, the Village wants to enlarge on this beginning. It should be mentioned in passing that living and working at Hancock for a period of time bites less deeply into the tight student budget than does research at libraries or institutions in high-priced metropolitan areas.

A project which takes on increased urgency with the passing of each year is the implementation of an oral history program. Near Hancock — indeed, near every Shaker settlement — there are still people who remember Shaker life as it was, but who have not committed their recollections to paper. The staff and trustees want to record their impressions while they are still alive.

Finally, we must remodel to obtain more space — space for books and manuscripts, space for tapes and microfilms, working space and, not least, space for a new microfilm reader.

Staff Requirements

So far, the Village has managed to function and to grow with a small paid staff and a dedicated group of volunteers. Capital funding is now needed to underwrite increased staff for supervision of an ever larger physical plant, an increased number of visitors, and an expansion in Village activity.

To administer an annual operating budget which exceeds one half million dollars, a full-time business manager is needed. Further, a concern with fire, security, and the ongoing maintenance of the Village require a full-time superintendent of buildings and grounds.

Future Restorations

"Buildings which get out of repair," counseled the Elders, "should be repaired soon, or taken away, as is most proper." Which, during their 170 years at Hancock, is just what the Shakers did. Many structures were damaged or destroyed by fire — a continual hazard to a community built out of wood and heated by wood. Others were dismantled when they outlived their usefulness. Still others were moved from one village to another and re-erected with adaptations for a different purpose in life.

As a result, it becomes impossible to recapture a moment in time and consider that moment as truly representative of the Shaker existence. In their building as in their agriculture and industrial work, they were innovators, always ready to revise, to adapt, to modernize. Keeping up with the times became, in itself, a Shaker tradition.

The Future of the City of Peace / 161

The Hancock Village of today has tried, with great attention to historical accuracy, to recreate a continuum of those 170 eventful years. No Shaker settlement could be considered complete, for example, without a meeting house, even though the village which the trustees purchased in 1960 no longer had such a building. They found a meeting house and moved it to Hancock, as described in the chapter on restorations.

It lies beyond our capabilities or intentions to reconstruct the physical appearance of the Village at all times during its long active life. But we do intend to capitalize on the restoration program which has already re-created so much of the essence of Shaker life.

This involves, first, completing work on buildings that are now partially restored. Priority goes to the Brick Dwelling, which has become a focal point for current Village activities. Repairs to the exterior masonry and brick work are mandatory. Cornices need rebuilding, shutters need to be replaced and the entire structure painted. Inside chimneys, walls and ceilings need plaster restoration; the building needs missing shelving and doors reconstructed as well as the replacement of the two great sliding wall partitions in the meeting room.

A home must be found, as well, for proper display of the Village's collection of horse-drawn carriages and tillage equipment. There is a Shaker carriage shed nearby which should be moved to a location adjacent to the barn complex and reconditioned for exhibiting this equipment.

Nor is the Village complete without an ash house used by the Shakers for storing wood and later coal ashes — an abundant supply of natural fertilizer which always found its way back into the land for the next growing season. Or a Shaker privy or two which provided another type of fertilizer often referred to as "nightsoil or poudrette."

From 1854 until the turn of the century, the Shakers had their own post office. The trustees and staff share the hope that a substation of the Pittsfield Post Office, to serve West Pittsfield, Hancock and Richmond, can again become active at the Village.

Good order — so important to the Shakers — exhorted brethren and sisters "to lay out, and fence all kinds of lots, fields and gardens, in a square form, where it is practicable." This was reinforced with a reminder to mend fences in the springtime, "for Zion is called to be a pattern of economy and order in all things."

In the spring of 1984, and for many springs thereafter, there will be fences to build and fences to mend. As restoration and research into history proceeds, those people charged with the legacy of the City of Peace must remember the need for economy and order in all things.

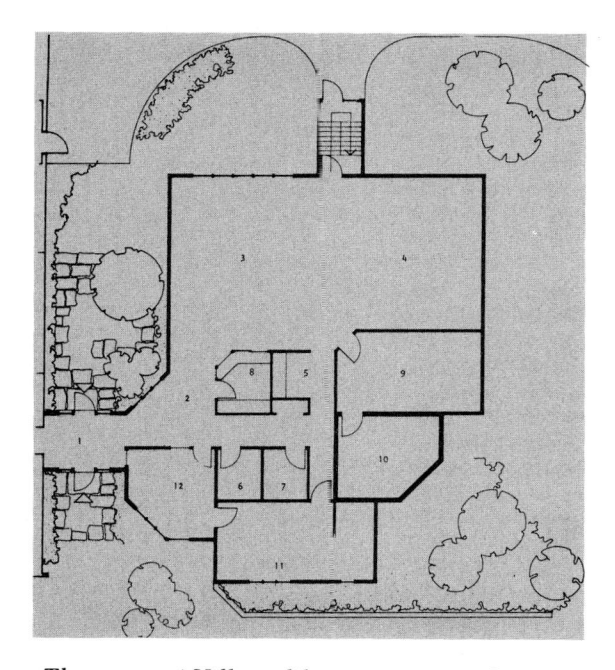

The present Village library occupies five rooms on the second floor of the Poultry House. Rather than remodel ths small building, the Trustees have committed themselves to raising $300,000 for a new library. This 11-room facility, an addition to the present Reception Center, will have shelf space for 10-12,000 volumes. There will also be a reading room, exhibition space and a conference room. It will be an expanded center for Shaker studies. The cost is included in the current $2 million fund-raising campaign.

162 / Hancock Shaker Village

CHRONOLOGY OF RESTORATION

1960: Shaker Community Inc. is formed to preserve Hancock Shaker Village. Edward D. Andrews appointed curator. Fund-raising effort brings in $100,000.

1961: Village opens to public on July 1. Sisters' Shop, Brethren's Shop, Brick Dwelling are available for visits.

1961 attendance 4,500.

1962: Poultry House is restored. Meeting House moved from Shirley, Mass., to Hancock.

1963: Wilbur Glover is appointed director of the Village.

1963 attendance 8,599

1964: "Kitchen Sisters" organized. Annual Shaker Kitchen Festival and the World's People's Dinners are inaugurated.

1964 attendance 11,000

1965: Eugene M. Dodd is appointed curator of the Village. Friends of Hancock Shaker Village organized. Eric Sloane heads "Save the Round Barn" Drive. $8,000 is raised on the "Save the Barn Day."

1965 atttendance 16,500

1966: The Village acquires the Mary Earle Gould Collection.

1966 attendance 19,000

1967: Machine Shop & Laundry, Ice House, Ministry Shop are restored. The Village is featured on NBC's "Today Show."

1967 attendance 22,160

1968: The Round Stone Barn is opened after restoration. Fall Shaker Breakfasts are inaugurated. A three-day conference on the cultural heritage of the Shakers is held.

1968 attendance 30,000

1969: Hancock Shaker Village is designated a National Historic Landmark.

1969 attendance 35,016

1970: John H. Ott is appointed curator of the Village. A Shaker exhibition travels to Expo '70 in Japan.

1970 attendance 39,000

1971: John Ott is named director of the Village.

1971 attendance 40,600

1972: Shaker exhibition presented at the Winter Antiques Show in New York.

1972 attendance 43,000

1973: Tan House is restored.

1973 attendance 45,371

1974: Shaker Bicentennial Year, with many television features on the Shakers. An exhibition of Shaker furniture and artifacts tours Europe.

1974 attendance 47,230

1975: Special exhibition at the Ellis Memorial Antiques Show in Boston.

1975 attendance 49,500

1976: U.S. Post Office issues bicentennial stamp commemorating the Shakers at Hancock.

1976 attendance 45,700 (unpaid attendance excluded here and for subsequent years)

1977: June Sprigg is appointed curator of the Village. Exhibitions are mounted at the State House in Boston and the William Benton Museum in Storrs, Conn. Hired Men's Shop is restored.

1977 attendance 46,900

1978:
1978 attendance 47,900

1979: "Art of the Shakers" exhibition opened in New York City. Capital Fund Drive raises $800,000 for remodeling barn complex and launching Community Industries Program. The Schoolhouse is rebuilt on its original site.

1979 attendance 49,058

1980: Opera: "The Singing Tree," is given its world premiere at Hancock. The First Fall Antique Show is held in the Round Stone Barn.

1980 attendance 49,600

1981: Restored barn complex opened, with an active Community Industries Program. Council of Friends of Hancock Shaker Village is organized. Second Antiques Show held in Round Stone Barn.

1981 attendance 49,887

1982: Third Annual Antiques Show held.

1982 attendance 52,944

1983: Hancock Shaker Village launches $2.5 million capital and endowment fund campaign. Jerry V. Grant succeeds John Ott as the Village's Director. Fourth Annual Antiques Show held.

1983 attendance 54,000

164 / Hancock Shaker Village

APPENDIX (TRUSTEES)

(D – Deceased; R – Resigned)

1960

Eldress Emma K. King   D
  Honorary Trustee
  Canterbury, NH

Edward D. Andrews   R
  First Curator
  Pittsfield, MA

David V. Andrews   R
  Vice President of Chase Manhattan Bank
  New York, NY

Faith Y. Andrews   R
  Pittsfield, MA

Laurence R. Connor   D
  President, Agricultural National Bank
  Pittsfield, MA

Charles R. Crimmin
  Attorney
  Pittsfield, MA

Stuart C. Henry
  Director, Berkshire Museum
  Pittsfield, MA

Robert S. Hibbard   D
  President, Stevenson & Co. (Ins.)
  Pittsfield, MA

Patricia Lynch (Mrs. Frank Faucett)
  The Berkshire Eagle
  Pittsfield, MA

Paul J. Major   R
  Business Manager, The Berkshire Eagle
  Pittsfield, MA

Amy Bess Miller
  Pittsfield, MA

Lawrence K. Miller
  Editor, The Berkshire Eagle
  Pittsfield, MA

Donald B. Miller   R
  Publisher, The Berkshire Eagle
  Pittsfield, MA

Margo Miller
  Reporter, The Boston Globe
  Boston, MA

Robert G. Newman
  Librarian, Berkshire Athenaeum
  Pittsfield, MA

Robert O. Parks   R
  Director, Smith College Museum of Art

Emily C. Rose
  New York City & Berkshire Co.

Milton C. Rose
  Attorney
  New York, NY

Frank O. Spinney   R
  Director, Old Sturbridge Village

Mrs. Edgar B. Stern   D
  New Orleans, LA

Thomas B. Hess   D
  Editor, Art News
  New York, NY

Philip Guyol   R
  Director, New Hampshire Historical Society

Carl P. Rollins   D
  Director, Yale University Press

Margaret D. Rollins   D
  New Haven, CT

Mario DePillis   R
  Professor, University of Mass.
  Amherst, MA

Bernard R. Carman   R
  The Berkshire Eagle
  Williamstown, MA

Edgar R. Baker   D
  Time-Life International
  New York, NY

S. Lane Faison
  Director, Williams College Museum of Art

Mrs. John M. Gilchrist   R
  (later on Advisory Board)

Charles D. Jackson   D
  Time, Executive Vice President

Charles R. Keller   R
  Professor, Williams College
  Williamstown, MA

Dorothy C. Miller
  Curator, Museum of Modern Art
  New York, NY

Prof. David Potter   R
  Professor, Yale University
  New Haven, CT

Edith Weyerhaeuser   R
  Duxbury, MA

Carl A. Weyerhaeuser
  Duxbury, MA

Catherine White   R
  New York, NY

Hon. Raymond S. Wilkins   D
  Supreme Court
  Boston, MA

John S. Williams   D
  President, Shaker Museum
  Old Chatham, NY

1961

Mrs. Malcolm G. Chace, Jr.
  Providence, RI

Frederick G. Crane   D
  Crane & Company
  Dalton, MA

1983

Thomas E. O'Connell   R
  President, Berkshire Community College

John McAndrew   D
  Director, Museum of Art, Wellesly College

1964

Mrs. Livingston Hall   R
  Great Barrington, MA

1966

Mrs. Ludwig Lederer
  New Lebanon, NY

Mrs. Robert Littell   D
  Tyringham, MA

Mr. Joseph D. Ryle
  New York, NY

Mr. Samuel G. Colt, Jr.   D
  Pittsfield, MA

1966

Eldress Gertrude M. Soule
  Honorary Trustee
  Canterbury, NH

1968

Mrs. Hamilton Kean (Mrs. Edgar R. Baker)
  New York, NY

Dr. Beatrice B. Berle
  Physician
  New York, NY (summer res. of Berk.)

Mrs. Robert S. Hibbard   R
  Richmond, MA

Mr. William V. Lawson
  New York, NY

1968

Mr. Peter Van S. Rice   R
  Treasurer, A.H. Rice Company
  Pittsfield, MA

1969

NO NEW TRUSTEES

1970

NO NEW TRUSTEES

1971

Terry Hallock
  Architect
  Pittsfield, MA

E. Ray Pearson
  Professor, Illinois Institute of Technology
  Chicago, IL

Mrs. Donald E. Richmond   R
  Southbury, CT

1972

Charles A. Weyerhaeuser
  Director, Duxbury Art Institute

William Henry Harrison IV
  Director, Museum at Fruitlands

Frederick L. Rath, Jr.
  National Park Service
  Washington, D.C.

Thomas F. Carrington
  President, Berkshire County Savings Bank

Douglas Bogart   R
  New York, NY

1973

C. Frederick Rudolph
  Professor American Studies
  Williams College

1977

Frederic H. Brandi   D
  Retired, Dillon Reed President

John Calkins
  Calkins Communications
  First National Bank
  Boston, MA

Mrs. James D. Hunter   R
  Williamstown, MA

Alastair Maitland   R
  Boston, MA

1978

Mrs. Henry A. Murray
  Cambridge, MA

Mrs. Edna J. Hirst
  New York, NY

Wendell Garrett
  Editor, Antiques Magazine
  New York, NY

David W. Murphy
  Stevenson & Co.
  Pittsfield, MA

1979

Richard S. Jackson, Jr.
  Lenox, MA

Robert L. Raley
  Architect
  Dover, DE

1980

Mrs. Arthur Paddock
  Pittsfield, MA

Samuel Boxer
  Retired Business Executive
  Pittsfield, MA

Frederick G. Crane, Jr.
  Crane & Company
  Dalton, MA

William H. Harrison IV
  Retired Director, Fruitlands Museum

Harriet Trainer
  New Lebanon, NY

Foster Trainer   D
  Retired Businessman
  New Lebanon, NY

1981

B. Carter White, Jr.
  President, Alliance Editions
  Richmond, MA

1982

Armand V. Feigenbaum
  General Systems Co.
  Pittsfield, MA

Donald S. Feigenbaum
  General Systems Co.
  Pittsfield, MA

Warden McL. Williams
  Waccabuc, NY

Mrs. Henry Cadwallader
  York Harbor, ME

John K. Howat
  New York, NY

1983

George Kramer
  New York, NY

Daniel A. Ford
  Pittsfield, MA

John Munro
  Pittsfield, MA

Joseph Duffy
  Pittsfield, MA

Susan Sweatland
  Pittsfield, MA

BIBLIOGRAPHY

Hancock Shaker Village Publications

The Village is listed as publisher for those publications issued under its imprint. It has participated in the others listed either through providing financial assistance, offering research assistance and facilities, or because a staff member is the author of a particular work.

Andrews, Edward Deming
    The American Shakers. (Pittsfield, Shaker Community Inc., 1961; 16 pp.)
    The Hancock Shakers: The Shaker Community at Hancock, Massachusetts 1780-1960. (Hancock, Hancock Shaker Community, Inc., 1961: 39 [1] pp., illus.)
    A Shaker meeting house and its builder. (Hancock, Shaker Community Inc., 1962; 15 pp.)

Desroche, Henri
    The American Shakers: from neo-Christianity to pre-socialism. Tr. by John Savacool. (Amherst, U. of Mass. Press, 1971, 357 pp., charts.)

Gordon, Beverly
    Shaker textile arts. (The University Press of New England, in cooperation with the Merrimac Valley Textile Museum and Shaker Community, Inc. 1980; 329 pp., illus.)

Hancock Shaker Village
    Hancock Shaker Village: its growing importance in preserving our American heritage. (Hancock, Shaker Community, Inc., 1979; 15 pp., illus.)
    Shaker Sweetmeats: a keepsake from Hancock Shaker Village. (Hancock, Shaker Community, Inc., 1965; [17] pp., illus.)

Mang, Karl und Eva, eds.
    Die Shaker: leben und producktion einer commune in der pionierzeit Amerikas. (Munchen, Die Neue Sammlung, 1974; 164 pp., illus.; also in English, French, Spanish and Danish.)

Miller, Amy Bess
    Hancock Shaker Village: The City of Peace. (Hancock, Hancock Shaker Village, 170 pp., illus.)
    Hancock Shaker Village: a consuming interest. (Pittsfield, Eagle Print Shop, 1983; 18 pp.)
    Shaker herbs: a history and a compendium. (N.Y., Clarkson Potter, 1976; 272 pp., illus.)
  and Persis Fuller, eds.
    The best of Shaker cooking. (N.Y., Macmillan, 1970, xix, 457 pp., illus.)

Ott, John Harlow
    Hancock Shaker Village: a guidebook and history. (Pittsfield, Shaker Community, Inc., 1976; 143 pp., illus.)

Pearson, Elmer R. and Julia Neal
    The Shaker image. (Preface by Walter Muir Whitehill, captions by Amy Bess Miller and John H. Ott; New York Graphic Society and Shaker Community, Inc., 1974; 190 pp., illus.)

Richmond, Colin Becket
    A collection of Shaker thoughts. (Syracuse, Brad. litho, 1976; 82 pp., illus.)
    From their hearts and hands: a treasury of Shaker poetry. (Syracuse, Brad. litho, 1974; 133 pp., illus.)
    Shaker 1973 calendar-journal. (Hastings-on-Hudson, N.Y., Morgan & Morgan, 1972; 64 pp., illus.)

Richmond, Mary L., comp.
    Shaker literature; a bibliography in two volumes. (Hancock, Shaker Community, Inc., 1977; 253, 338 pp.)

Sprigg, June
    By Shaker hands. (N.Y., Knopf, 1975, 212 vii pp., illus. by author.)

Works in Progress
    Shaker furniture makers. (The University Press of New England, Hanover, N.H., to be published in 1985)

INDEX

Abrams, George, 80
Allhusen, Helen, 98
Anderson, Cheryl, 130, 148
Andrews, David V., 20, 26, 28, 36, 40
Andrews, Mrs. David V., 20, 26, 28, 36
Andrews, Edward Deming, 18, 20, 95, 100, 101, 103 121, 128, 139, 140, 145, 146
Andrews, Mrs. Edward Deming, 18, 20, 95, 100, 145
Annin, Katharine H., 47
Arruda, Ellen, 94
Austin, See Hayden
Baal-Teshuva, Aviva, 142
Babarczy, E. Mario, 80, 122
Baker, Roy W., 21, 28, 33, 55
Barber, John Warner, 26
Barber, Dr. Russell, 125, 126
Barker, James Madison, 27
Barker, John, 20
Barker, Sister R. Mildred, 31, 34, 142
Basting, Elder Louis, 80, 107
Bates, Issachar, 140
Beard, James, 112
Beinecke, Edward, 137
Beinecke, Walter, 137
Beinecke, Frederick W. "Fritz", 41, 47, 82, 137
Beinecke, Mrs. Frederick W. (Carrie), 41
Beinecke, William S., 82
Belden, Elizabeth, 19, 20
Belden, Ricardo, 16, 18-19, 57-58
Belden, Sister Emoretta, 98
Berle, Dr. Beatrice B., 108
Black, Mary C., 127
Blanchard, Elder Grove, 100
Blinn, Elder Henry Clay, 34, 89, 91, 141
Blodgett, Mrs. Thomas H. (Margaret), 41, 137
Boice, Avis Drake, 75, 110
Bolger, William F., 128
Bona, Danny, 80
Borden, Gail, 112
Bragg, Laura M., 20
Brewer, Priscilla, 142
Bronson, Hannah, 120
Brownlow, Lady, 79
Brownlow, Lord Richard, 123
Cahill, Dorothy Miller, 20, 137
Calkins, John, 109, 131
Carman, Bernard R., 25
Carmon, Eileen, 139, 155
Carver, Sister Amelia J., 157
Cashman, Mrs. J.M., 98
Catlin, Janet Green, 131
Chamberlain, Samuel, 140
Chace, Mrs. Malcolm G., Jr., 95
Claiborne, Craig, 142
Clark, Fanny G., 97, 98
Clark, Phillip L., 28, 85, 132, 134, 146
Clarke, Andrew, 128

Cleveland, Bryce T., 128
Clough, Henry T., 98
Collins, Eldress Sarah, 16, 20
Colt, Samuel G., 123
Colt, Mrs. Samuel G., 123
Conant, Lorring, 21
Conforth, John, 142
Congdon, Arthur, 128
Conlin, Mary Lou, 127
Connor, Laurence R., 23, 27
Conroy, Francis, 79, 80, 156
Conte, Silvio O., 127, 128
Cook, Mrs. Harold E., 100
Corcoran, Robert J., 88
Crane, Mrs. Bruce, 41
Crane, Winthrop M., Jr., 28, 100, 137
Crimmin, Charles R., 23, 25
Crook, Sister Ida, 23, 71, 97
Cummings, Abbott Lowell, 38, 40
Dahlen, Martha, 116
Dahm, Sister Mary, 18, 26, 71, 95
Davenport, Tom, 125
Davis, R.H., 77, 82
Deming, Elder William, 71, 74
DePillis, Mario, 127
DesRoche, Henri, 140
Dickens, Charles, 31, 110, 130
Dixon, William Hepsworth, 94
Doane, Albert G., 36
Dodd, Eugene Merrick, 123, 146-147
Drury, Mary, 155
Dupont, Henry Francis, 133
Dunbar, Mrs. Davis T., 20
Duval, Frances Persip, 89, 125, 154
Duyckinck, Evert, 43
Eckel, Rev. Malcolm W., 30, 40
Edwards, Jonathan, 11
Elam, Sister Aida, 154
Emerson, Ralph Waldo
Emlen, Robert, 142
Estabrook, Eldress Fannie, 18, 26
Fahey, Frederick J., 36
Faison, Prof. S. Lane, 21, 107
Feld, Stuart P., 130
Fellows, John Hay, 130
Ferris, Nancy, 146
Field, David Dudley, 43
Filley, Dorothy, 142
Finkelpearl, Katherine, 142
Flint, Charles, 100
Flynt, Henry N., 29, 133
Flynt, Mrs. Henry N., 133
Ford, Henry, 133
Foster, Stephen C., 100
Fowles, Mr. & Mrs. Edward, 123
Francese, Peter, 86
Fromman, Louis, 140
Fujikami, Bro. Peter, 122
Fuller, Andrew W., 146
Fuller, George A. Company, 59
Fuller, Persis Wellington, 74, 110, 112, 116, 125, 137, 140

Fuss, Walter, 23
Garrett, Wendell, 100
Gebhard-Gourgaud, Eva B., 82
Gilchrist, Mrs. John A., 20, 21
Glover, Wilbur H., 146
Gordon, Beverly, 142
Gould, Mary Earle, 63, 97, 147
Grant, Jerry V., 100, 147
Granville, Henrietta, 146
Griffin, Donald F., 128
Guerrieri, Anthony, 86
Guyol, Philip, 21
Hall, Sister Frances, 18, 19
Hall, Margaret H., 28-29
Hawthorne, Nathaniel, 19, 31, 43, 116, 130
Hayden, Sister Olive, 77, 121
Hallock, Terry, 28, 33, 40, 41, 47, 55, 60, 77, 85, 89, 146
Hamilton, Beverly, 154
Hancock, John, 29
Hansis, Roma, 154
Harrington, Thomas F., 149
Harrison, William Henry, 140
Hazzard, Mary, 40
Held, Conrad, 40
Henry, Stuart C., 25
Herold, Donald, 122
Herron, Robert, 100
Heyniger, C. Lambert, 25
Hirschl, Norman, 130
Hitchcock, Prof. Henry Russell, 20
Hocknell, John, 11
Holland, Josiah Gilbert, 29, 43
Hollister, Alonzo G., 98
Howard, Arthur A., 101
Howard, Mrs. Arthur A., 101
Howard, Frank, 101
Howard, Mrs. Frank, 101
Howland, Richard H., 21
Johnson, Mrs. Lyndon B., 131
Johnson, Moses, 34, 36
Johnson, Patrick, 131
Johnson, Theodore E., 142
Joline, John, 58
Kastle, Leonard, 116
Kaufman, Edgar Jr., 41
Keller, Prof. Charles R., 130
Kelly, Martha, 120
Kennedy, John F., 33
Kidder, Eli, 98
Kimball, Robert B., 137
King, Eldress Emma B., 19, 23, 25, 26, 43-44, 56, 85, 97, 105, 108, 130, 140
Knoepel, Penny, 116
Knopf, Alfred, 148
Kouwenhoven, John H., 154
Kramer, Hilton C., 130
Kring, Rev. Walter D., 38, 40
Lafayette, Marquis de, 130
Lassiter, William Laurence, 137
Lawson, Elder Ira, 80

Lederer, D. Veola, 126, 131
Lee, Ann, 11, 29, 74, 77, 101, 104, 108, 123, 125 127, 133
Lee, John, 11
Lee, William, 12
Lemieux, Leo, 86, 146
Lessom, Jeanne, 116
Lincoln, Leo L., 128
Lilly, Joshua, 48
Lipman, Jean, 20
Little, Betram K., 27
Little, Nina Fletcher, 130
Lindsay, Eldress Bertha, 31, 107, 126, 127
Low, George D., 109
Lynch, Patricia A., 25
MacLean, J.P., 139
McCain, Bob, 154
McClintock, Norman O., 146
Mackie, C.E., 146
Major, Paul J., 25
Matthews, M.D., 103
Matthews, Mrs. M.D., 103
Mattoon, H. Gleason, 27, 47, 79, 91, 94
May, Gilbert, 80
Meader, Robert F.W., 103, 127, 142
Melville, Herman, 43, 116
Merton, Thomas, 101, 145
Melcher, Marguerite F., 140
Mele, Bonnie, 154
Mele, Pat, 154
Miller, Amy Bess Williams, 25, 36, 40, 41, 47, 95, 97, 100, 107, 112, 116, 125, 126, 127, 128, 130, 131, 132, 137, 139, 140, 141
Miller, Donald B., 20, 98
Miller, Dorothy (Mrs. Holger Cahill), 21, 23, 95
Miller, Lawrence K., 20, 21, 23, 25, 40, 95, 100, 130
Miller, Margo, 25
Miller, Marc C., 146
Miller, (Mr.) Kelton B., 16
Moon, Daniel H., 38
Moon, Maud Mary Olin, 38
Morgan, Helen M., 38
Morse, Richard A., 21, 23, 27
Murray, Dr. Henry A., 117
Myers, Frederic M., 19, 23
Neal, Mary Julia, 16, 141, 142
Neale, Eldress Emma J., 16, 109
Neale, Sister Sadie, 16
Newman, Robert G., 25
Newton, Vincent, 97
Nickles, Ed, 142
Nolan, Joseph H., 128
Nordstrom, Jane, 116
Ott, John Harlow, 55, 60, 79, 82, 85, 86, 125, 128, 130, 131, 132, 140, 142, 147, 148, 154
Ott, Lili, 131, 142-143
Page, Virginia, 28
Parego, Charles, 156
Parego, Mrs. Charles, 156
Parks, Robert O., 95
Patterson, Daniel W., 127

Pictrowski, Walter, 132, 146, 156
Peck, Clifford, 79
Pearson, Elmer R. "Ray," 141, 142
Peterson, Charles, 27, 28
Piercy, Caroline B., 74
Pike, Kermit J., 127
Piraino-Molevoet, Elaine, 142
Popperliers, John C., 127
Porter, Burt, 116
Porter, Daniel, 127
Potter, Clarkson N., 141
Randall, Benjamin, 11
Ravenswaay, Charles van, 127
Rensselaer, Steven van IV, 11
Rettalick, Frederick D., 107
Richmond, Mary L., 127, 139
Robinson, Charles Edson, 117
Rockefeller, John D., Jr., 133
Rollins, Carl Purlington, 20, 26, 139, 140
Rollins, Mrs. Carl P. (Margaret), 20, 26, 40, 139, 140
Root, Printers, 82
Rose, Milton, C., 20, 21
Rose, Mrs. Milton C., 20, 21
Ross, Charlie, 18-19
Rourice, Constance, 143
Rubenstein, Phyllis, 155, 156
Ruzicka, Rudolph, 128
Ryle, Joseph D., 132
Sanborn, Mrs. Bruce, 28, 36, 40
Sanborn, Maud Moon Weyerhaeuser (Mrs. Bruce), 38 123, 137
Sanborn, Bruce, 40, 137
Sarle, Helena, 141
Savacool, John K., 140
Sawyer, John E., 131
Scherer, John, 142
Schwerdtfeger, Gus, 100
Schwerdtfeger, Alice, 100
Seddon, Charles, 82
Sears, Miss Clara Endicott, 107, 141
Sheehan, John J., 23
Sheeler, Mr. Charles, 97
Sheeler, Mrs. Charles, 97
Simmons, Adelma G., 132
Sinclair, Mrs., 116
Sloane, Eric, 47, 123, 137
Sloper, Archibald K., 31
Sloper, Mrs. Archibald K., 31
Smith, Alice, 20
Smith, Mrs. Frank C., 100
Smith, Starbuck, 89
Soule, Eldress Gertrude M., 23, 31, 34, 97, 104, 105, 126, 127, 128
Spinney, Frank O., 20, 21
Sprigg, June, 28, 130, 142, 148, 149
Stanley, Abraham, 11
Stell, Elizabeth, 94
Stephens, Alice Barber, 40
Stern, Edgar B., 41, 137
Stern, Mrs. Edgar B., (Edith), 47, 79, 91, 105, 137, 146

Summerson, Sir John, 29-30
Symonds, Alfred C., III, 146
Talbot, William, 127
Tallott, Josiah Jr., 80
Taylor, Leila S., 75-76, 104, 137
Thielker, Alan, 146
Thompson, Charles, 141
Tobin, James, 60, 79
Trainor, Foster B.,Jr.,
Udall, Stewart, 123
Underwood, Bayard, 142
Upton, Prof. Charles, 97, 98
Upton, Mrs. Charles, 97, 98
Valentine, Robert, 98
Van Doren, Mark, 145
Victoreen, Walfrid T., 97
Viner, Janet, 125
Volpe, John A., 36
Vosburgh, Francis, 146
Walchenbach, Dorothy, 109
Wall, Eldress Gertrude, 107
Wall, Sister Miriam, 31, 107, 126, 127, 130, 154
Wardley, James, 11
Wardley, Jane, 11
Weber, Melva, 91
Webb, Mrs. J. Watson, 133
Wells, Sister Jennie, 74
Westhoven, Thomas N., 128
Wertzburger, Janet, 112
Weyerhaeuser, Carl A., 20, 123, 130
Weyerhaeuser, Mrs. Carl A., 20
Weyerhaeuser, Charles A., 130
Whitaker, James, 157
White, Eldress Anna, 75-76, 104, 139
Whitefield, George, 11
Whitehill, Walter Muir, 29, 33, 116, 141, 146-147
Wiggins, Kate Douglas, 40
Wilkins, Raymond S., 28, 107
William, August W., 127
Williams, John S., 20
Wilson, Brother Delmer, 103
Winchester, Harold P., 30
Winters, William F., 20
Wright, Elder Grove, 100
Wyatt-Brown, Bertram, 127
Yoder, Don, 127
Young, I.N., 140
Youngs, Isaac N., 98, 128
Youngs, Benjamin S., 140